T0149634

I'm The Plug

I'm The Plug

Trying to Fly with One Wing, Volume Two

MOE LOVE

I'M THE PLUG
TRYING TO FLY WITH ONE WING, VOLUME TWO

iUniverse books may be ordered through booksellers or by contacting:

iUniverse
1663 Liberty Drive
Bloomington, IN 47403
www.iuniverse.com
1-800-Authors (1-800-288-4677)

ISBN: 978-1-5320-6481-4 (sc)
ISBN: 978-1-5320-6482-1 (e)

Library of Congress Control Number: 2018914751

Print information available on the last page.

iUniverse rev. date: 12/12/2018

Dedicated to
Arthur Eutsey (1951 - 2018)

Chapter One

Unck had pled guilty to the charge of manslaughter and received a five to fifteen-year sentence. He served his term and had been released from prison. His only obstacle he had preventing him from returning to his previous glory, was his two-year parole obligations.

Unck killed his sister in-law for having the audacity to confront him about pimping her daughter. His wife, who was fondly known as Auntie, stayed beside the man she loved, despite the fact she witnessed him open her sister's throat with a straight razor. Her world, and entire family was torn apart by the tragic fatal incident. Her only family member to continue to love and support her unconditionally, was her brother. He did so under the constant staunch objections from numerous family members. He loved her so dearly, he couldn't imagine living a life which didn't include his older sister, so he refused to do so.

Unck also had a sister named Etta. She was an amazing woman. Tall, beautiful, classy, and eloquent are some of the adjectives that come to my mind whenever I'm trying to describe her. Her hair was long, black, and wavy, as well as smooth as silk to the touch. Her skin tone was that of rich dark chocolate. She processed powerful Indian features, with a strikingly beautiful profile. Her body was full of the curves that delighted all potential lovers, and suitors. She had huge breast and was not shy when it came to her cleavage being displayed. With practically no waistline, and the hips, ass, and shapely legs to match, she was, without any doubt, the personification of sexy.

She was very informed and smart, but another word used to describe this amazing woman, was forgiving. Just as Unck had opened the throat of his sister in-law with a straight razor, he had also used the same method to open his niece's throat, which happened to have been his sister Etta's daughter, Regina. Regina survived the brutal attack, and eventually joined her mother in the forgiveness of her uncle. I found it mind boggling. Many felt Etta and Regina had taken a leave of absence from their senses, while others thought them to be amazingly stupid. The truth was, much simpler. The man was a pure charmer.

I sat in his living room talking to this legend, and found it exhilarating. He allowed me to ask questions whenever there was something said that I didn't understand and asked me questions which tested my degree of knowledge of the game. Most of the question I answered correctly, but there were some I got completely wrong. It was a win, win situation for me, because even though I may have answered the question incorrectly, I learned what the answers should have been, and thus received the pearls of knowledge and wisdom.

He eventually asked me what I wanted. I answered, "I want to be the richest dope man to ever sell dope in the city of Newport." He promised to do everything in his power to help me to realize that dream, and he would start by introducing me to every plug he knew, as his son. I asked when we would get started, and he asked, in a matter of fact tone, "What the fuck is wrong with right now?"

He promptly picked up the telephone and called City cab. When he hung up the receiver to the phone, he looked deeply into my eyes, and asked again, "What is it you want?" I answered once again, "To be the richest dope man to ever sell dope in this city!" "Well come on." he ordered. "Let's get busy." Soon after, the cab arrived, and we were on our way.

To my surprise, we went to the Player's Club. It was a gangster's social club that catered to a members-only cliental. If you weren't a member, you had to be escorted by a member, to be permitted entrance. I was escorted by the most popular, respected figure in town.

This place was extravagant. Everywhere you looked was pleasing to the senses. I found the aromas of incense, perfumes and colognes, as well as the smells of the different types of foods being prepared, intoxicating!

There were luxurious textures of silk, satin, and velour in red everywhere you looked, accented with gold paint. Even the floors were finished in a thick red shag carpet. Up against one of the walls, there was a long fully stocked bar, which stretch from one end of the room to the other. It too was covered with different textures of red materials and accented with gold paint.

After introducing me to everyone in attendance as his son, he stretched his hand out for my assistance, as he climbed on top of the pool table. "Check this shit out everybody..." he began. "I'm going to step inside the office for a bit, and while I'm in there, it will give you guys the opportunity to show me just how grateful you are for my safe return. It would be wise,

3

and appreciated, if I was to find a sizable donation on the table when I come out."

Once again, he stretched his hand out for my assistance, as he climbed down to the floor. I watched as he strutted to the office while Miles Davis' song entitled, So What, played in the background. It was like a scene from a motion picture. I watched in amazement as they all walked proudly to the pool table and threw huge rolls of bills on top of it. I had seen large amounts of money before, but they were the proceeds from robberies, or drug deals. This was much different. This was not some type of shake down, or intimidation, seeded in threats. No, this was an act of love and respect, as well admiration. I found it hard to understand the love and forgiveness that was heaped upon this man who had terrorized his family. I learned that night that I understood very little about life, or about Unck.

Unck came out the back room and retrieved the bounty from the table. He told me he was going to spend the night there gambling as he handed me a couple of hundred dollars. "You can go catch up with your crowd youngster. It's grown folks time now." He said as he chuckled and walked away.

I hadn't touched base with June Bug, so I caught a cab to his house. We had to brainstorm. Somehow, we had to come up with an idea that would net the necessary capital to finance a new business venture. He answered his door with a broad smile. There was a glow of optimism everywhere.

"I think I've found the way for us to get the money to buy a sack." He proudly stated before I was completely in the house. "We're going to rob a bank!" were the words he spoke after he closed the door. "Mutha Fucka, you done lost yo mind? You don't want to fuck with the Feds!" I warned him. I warned him because the old folks had always warned us about the Feds. I was only repeating what I'd heard, and not speaking from actual experience, which June pointed out.

"What makes them so muthafuckas special, huh?" he asked. "They're human, and make mistakes, just like the rest of us. They put their pants on one leg at a time, just like the rest of us. They must eat, sleep, shit and piss, just like the rest of us. Besides, if they were so dam smart, how come more people get away with robbing banks than there are people who get caught? Answer me that?" It was obvious that he was very serious about the idea of our crew robbing a bank.

He had been talking to Fat James, and insisted we leave right then, and that I accompany him to Fat James' apartment. Fat James had lost a lot of weight, but not the name. He was a tall, slim built, dark skinned brother. He had the reputation of being a sharp dresser, but more importantly, he was well known for robbing banks.

Fat James opened the door of his apartment and greeted us with a genuine smile. After welcoming us, he invited us to take a seat in his living room. A beautiful young sharply dressed woman was sitting in the living room, with a small child. It was as though one hundred percent of her attention was devoted to Fat James. When their eyes locked, he tilted his head slightly in the direction of what appeared to be their bedroom. The entire scene was a bit strange to me, because she intentionally avoided making eye contact with me, like prostitutes do when they are trying to avoid being caught out of pocket.

She quickly stood up, and gathered a few things, before placing her little girl on her hip. Her toenails, and fingernails were manicured in an attention demanding deep red. Her skin tone was like a newly polished copper penny, and she had strong Indian features. Her hair was long, dark and wavy. So long in fact, that the braided pony tail she wore, hung well passed her voluptuous buttocks. You couldn't help but notice how long and shapely her legs were, as she hurriedly strutted towards the bedroom. Once she reached her destination she gently and quietly closed the door.

Fat James had successfully robbed eight banks in the New Port metropolitan area. That night he gave June Bug and I a crash course in "hitting jugs", as he called it. He had been a one-man operation and was content to reap what he could from a single teller. Now he had bigger aspirations. He wanted to hit all the tellers, as well as the vault. He explained in detail why it was impossible to do, without a crew.

"We'll have to think like a team, move like a team, and execute like a team, in order to be successful." He continued, "I know the police routes and schedules in this precinct. We'll have to be in and out in under five minutes, tops. The way the escape route is set up, we will be long gone, before the nearest squad car can respond. If we're careful not to draw any unnecessary attention to ourselves as we are leaving, we'll soon be back at my apartment without anyone knowing which direction we were headed, or what matter of transportation was used.

We decided right then and there, our next job would be a well, planned, bank robbery. We would gather the entire crew the next day to have a meeting, for the purpose of planning a bank robbery. An electric charge surged through me. I had never robbed a bank before. Whenever I thought of bank robbery, I thought of Thomasine and Bushrod, Dillinger, Bonnie and Clyde, Jesse James, Pretty Boy Floyd…ect. One bank robbery would not have put me in the same category as the historical individuals I've mentioned, however, once I've robbed a bank, I will be considered a bank robber.

I had June Bug dropped me off over my mother's house. I didn't have a woman or any special place I wanted to go. My mother's divorce from my father was final now. Normally I would have visited my brother, Albert's house. He had moved out and gotten his own place around the corner from our mother's house. My brothers Sonny and Anderson still lived with my mother during that time, as did my sisters Pandora, Rudine, and Marilyn. I missed them horribly. This was the perfect opportunity to spend some family time with them, without all the extra drama that existed between me and my father.

When I got out the car, I could hear loud music coming from across the street. Al Green was singing "For the Good Times", and the lights in Biggum's house were on. I felt a strong tug at my heart strings when I recognized the voice crying out to me. "What type of bird don't fly?" she asked. It was Marty. My true love. She had problems with our age difference. Not me. I was so deeply in love with her, she could have taken complete advantage of me should she had taken the notion to do so, but she never did. It was because she was just as deeply in love with me as I was with her, that she had never so much as taken me for granted.

She was sitting on the front porch all alone, in the shadows. Her shinny hair appeared to be a rich mid-night blue, as it reflected the light of the moon. She smiled, and the diamond that sat in the middle of her one gold tooth, sparkled, and literally lit my entire world.

The closer I got to her, the more exhilarating the sweet

fragrance of her perfume made me feel. She was sipping on a big mouth Mickey's malt liquor, and in the mood for flirting. When I took her into my arms to give her a hug, she held on to me so long without speaking, I began to believe something was wrong. As she looked deeply into my eyes, I could see the genuine love and joy she held in her heart. She never asked me why I did the things I did. She simply relished in my company and basked in the joy of my return. Then she kissed me in a way she had never kissed me before. When I compared that kiss to all the other kisses, it paled in comparison. That's when I realized what the difference was. All the other kisses were for me. This was the first time she had kissed me, seeking personal satisfaction.

It was obvious that she loved me just as much as I loved her, so I asked why we couldn't be together. She stared in my eyes as though she were determined to make me understand. "We are not ready yet. I just brought a spanking brand-new Mark IV, and I'm ready to have some serious fun.

Your name is ringing, and you can tell by the interest the ladies are expressing, your hands are about to be full! You're young, tall, black, fine, and exciting. There's a lot you need to experience before you decide to settle down, and you need to do it with someone your own age. If you still want this old lady after you learn about life, we'll talk about it then, but in the meantime, let's just have some fun!"

We had a long talk and became a lot closer. I understood a lot of things after our conversation that night. She was right about our age difference being a hindrance. She wanted to do the things that came with maturing. None of those things interest me. I enjoyed the night life, bar hopping from one club to the next. She had been clubbing for so many years, she was tired of the night life. I loved running the streets seeking fun. She enjoyed making the home so much fun and comfortable, you wouldn't want to leave, and if you did leave, you couldn't wait to get back. She was a mother with responsibilities. I was a free spirit with absolutely no obligations or responsibilities. I understood completely. She was right. We both needed more time to live, to grow, and sort things out. We sat on the porch and talked until dawn. It was an amazing night, and the sunrise thrilled us with its' majestic beauty.

The following day, we all gathered at Fat James' apartment to discuss the possibility of doing a bank job. The entire crew was in attendance, which included Obie, JB, June Bug, and Cat. That made six of us, and we were all seasoned and tested stick-up men. Fat James was the only one with experience robbing banks, but there were no doubts in any of our minds about our ability to successfully complete such a potentially profitable job. We were thrilled by the possibility of this being our first step to becoming seasoned bank robbers.

Fat James girl's name was Hope. While we were having our meeting, some of her friends came by to visit her. There was about six of them, and they all were gorgeous. One of them was a strikingly beautiful red bone, and she wore a huge, curly, blond afro hairdo like it was a crown. She was short but thick in all the right places. She had a big rear end, and a small, tight waistline. She wore a mini skirt, which showed off her big shapely legs.

She was so pretty I found it beyond difficult to not stare at her. I also noticed she was openly staring at me. It made chills run up and down my spine for her to stare at me in that manner. We were staring at each other, even though we were in separate rooms. She was in the room with the ladies, and I was in the room with the fellas.

We passed a few marijuana joints between each other and traded a few hilarious war stories. We got quiet when we overheard the girls talking loudly about what they would do if they found out their man was cheating. The redbone never took her eyes off me when it was her turn to voice her opinion. As she spoke she never looked away. It was as though she were speaking directly to me when she answered, "I would never leave my man, or breakup with my man if I found out he had another woman. I'm family orientated. Besides, why would I lay down and allow her to keep him, all to herself? It's not going to be that easy.

I was impressed by her answer. It wasn't what I expected to hear, but it was impressive all the same. All the other girls were explaining how badly they would go off on their guy, but not the redbone. What she was saying was completely the opposite of what the others were saying.

There was no shame in her game. When she had finished giving her answer, she slowly strolled up to me, and said, "Hi sweetie. My name is Destiny. I'm really digging you. Can we talk?" I patted my thigh, indicating my invitation for her to have a seat on my lap. She quickly sat down, and our first, lengthy, in depth conversation began.

Destiny's boyfriend had been murdered almost a year earlier, and she was ready to get on with her life. She was nineteen years old and looking for a man. She didn't want a square man. She wanted a man who was in the game and didn't mind making his woman get up off her ass and get paid. "I have the tendency to get lazy, so I need a nigga that's gonna stay in my ass. You know? Push me!" were her exact words.

We talked for quite a while, before Fat James interrupted, and reminded us of the purpose for the gathering. "Please excuse us ladies, we still have some business we must discuss. I had been so engrossed in the conversation I was having with Destiny, I hadn't noticed everyone had coupled off. The ladies excused themselves, and we continued with our meeting.

We were filled in on Fat James' plan to rob the National Bank. He gave detailed explanations for every part of his plan. His planning was so thorough, it included police routes. By the time we had adjourned our meeting, we all knew our assignments, and what our responsibilities would be. We were going to rob the bank at ten o'clock the next morning.

It was getting late, so Fat James suggested we retire, and get rested up. I asked Destiny for a number I could use to contact her, but she informed me she was moving in with Fat James and Hope, so I could drop by any time I wanted. She was staring at my lips as though she wanted me to kiss her. I wanted to kiss her too, so I followed my gut instincts, and tried to kiss her. I was surprised when she pulled me closer and slid her tongue inside of my mouth. The fragrance of her perfume filling my nostrils, accompanied with her sexual energy, was more than I'd expected to encounter. I had been caught totally off guard, and this chick was melting my heart. I found myself falling and falling hard.

I had June Bug drop me off over my brother's house, which was around the corner from my mother's house. That night I slept on the floor. I tossed and turned with excitement the entire night. I felt like a child on Christmas eve, waiting for Santa to arrive. Finding sleep was far more difficult than I anticipated.

Chapter Two

That following morning, I was awakened by the morning sun, and the blaring of the horn from June Bug's car. When I stepped outside, I saw Cat sitting in the passenger's seat. Obie was driving his car, which was parked behind June Bug's car, and JB was parked behind Obie's car, in his parent's Buick Electra.

If everything had gone according to plan, and it appeared so, Cat will have stolen a car from a local factory the night before and hid it near Fat James' apartment. The car won't be missed, but more importantly, it wouldn't be reported stolen until after the shift had changed. By then, it will have fulfilled its' purpose. That was the car we would use to do the job, then once we've counted and split the loot, we would split up, and leave in the other cars, headed in different directions.

They were quite early. I didn't mind, and I understood. I told them to give me a minute to freshen up, and I would be right out. Excitement, and a nervous tension filled the air. It was amazing me where my life's journey was taking me. Here I was, standing before the threshold of yet another fork in my road. I felt this day would be like no other. It certainly was starting out right.

When we arrived at Fat James' apartment, to our shock and amazement, we found the door barely hanging on its' hinges.

We immediately drew our weapons and made eye contact with one another. From that point on, all communications was done through our eyes, or sign language. Being the established enforcer, I always lived as though I had a death wish. I positioned myself at the entrance, to ensure I'd be the first to encounter whatever may be lying in wait.

I gently pushed the door aside, as I called out to Fat James. The door slowly, and quietly opened. Although we could clearly hear Hopes' voice answering, as she called out to us, it still wasn't clear what was going on, so we pressed forward.

This time I called out to Hope, just as she was coming from the bedroom. Her eyes were bloodshot red and swollen. Her tears were flowing, as she struggled to speak between each breathtaking sob. Something horrible had happened, and it became blatantly obvious that it would be necessary to calm her down before we be able find out what was going on.

Destiny came from the bedroom and began comforting Hope. Once she had calmed her down a bit, Hope began to speak. "The Federal Marshalls kicked our door in, at about seven o'clock this morning. There were so many of them, it was unbelievable. They were well groomed white men. Every single one of them were dressed in suites and ties. They were also very polite. They show us several pictures of Fat James robbing banks, just before they read him his rights and arrested him. They told him he was going away for a very long time."

Destiny stood near the bedroom's entrance, with an expression of bewilderment on her face. We made eye contact, and I could tell from the look in her eyes, her world had once again been turned upside down.

We were caught in a dilemma. Fat James was the one with the knowledge and experience. When he was taken into custody, so was the vast majority of our knowledge of hitting jugs. Should we continue as planned, and hit the jug without Fat James, or face the fact that we were far too inexperienced to attempt such a feat, without his guidance.

After a lengthy conversation, we all agreed. We didn't have enough experience to do the job. Fat James had made some serious mistakes. One of the mistakes he made, was not utilizing disguises. That proved to be the error which brought about his capture. I thought out loud, "I wonder how many other mistakes he has made that we were unaware of." That sealed the deal. The job was called off, and we would continue to do our own thing. The only problem we had, which prohibited us from continuing our arrangement with our connection, was the need for financing.

There was a liquor store on Vinewood we once had planned to rob. That was before we stopped robbing commercial businesses. I suggested we hit that store right then, since our plans to hit the jug had been diverted. It was the most logical thing to do. We had already cased this store, and we had precise detailed plans already in place. Everyone agreed. We merely had to refresh ourselves with the plans and map out an escape route.

This particular store was an extremely difficult store to rob. As a matter of fact, although there had been several attempts made, the store had never been successfully robbed. Slim used to plan all the robberies I participated in, and he once told me, because of the way the store was set up, it would take a team of seasoned stick up men, with perfect timing, to successfully pull off a robbery of this magnitude. The yield would be high, but so was the risk. Every time an attempt had been made to rob the store, there were devastating results. Someone always got shot, and it was never an employee.

The way the store was sit up, the manager worked the check cashing counter, where the liquor was also sold, to your left near the entrance. Every time anyone had been shot during a robbery attempt, it was always by this trigger-happy manager. There were three aisles with cash registers to the right. The one closest to the door, and directly across from the check cashing counter, was always manned by a man, and he was always armed. The other two aisles were manned by beautiful young foreign women whom barely spoke broken English. They were no threat, but the sum of money in their cash registers would be huge. Slim insisted the drop had to be gotten on both men simultaneously, and that would disarm the market. There was a butcher behind the meat counter, but he was not armed. There were always customers walking up and down the aisles shopping for groceries, and any one of them could take a notion to become a hero, which could cause trouble for us.

My assignment was the most dangerous, and I wouldn't have it any other way. I had to get the drop on the manager and disarm him, and Obie had to get the drop on the man at the cash register and disarm him. If either of us hesitated the other one's back wouldn't be covered, and they would be shot. I was more than willing to take the mangers life, if he offered any resistance. Our lives depended on me not hesitating to take the manager out, should he have plans that didn't include complying with my orders. This foreign man had shot so many brothers, I was practically itching to blast his ass to the afterlife at the very first opportunity.

June Bug would be the first to enter the store, then position himself near the line of the cash register where the man was working. Cat and JB would enter next, and immediately go to the aisles with shelves of groceries. Once June Bug saw me and Obie in position to get the drop, he would blow a whistle. He wanted to fire a shot in the floor, but the rest of us were against it. It was my contention that if a shot was heard, the trigger-happy manager might go for his weapon, and whomever had the quickest draw, would be the determining factor. I felt we should use a whistle to assure us of the element of surprise. While everyone will be wondering why this idiot was blowing his whistle inside the store, we will be drawing our weapons, and thereby disarming this difficult to rob liquor store.

We would leave from Obie's house in the stolen car and return to the abandoned house next door. We informed Hope of our plans to return later that day. Destiny insisted that I give my word to return. I did so, and to my surprise she seemed quite pleased with my willingness to comply with her request. She gave me a big hug and held on to me for what seemed like a long time, before eventually releasing me. "Please be careful. I need someone like you in my life." she said. I swear it took every bit of my strength to tear myself away from her, but I did.

Everything worked out just as planned. The delivery men were a bonus. We emptied all the cash registers, as well as the safe. JB and Hawk robbed every customer shopping in the aisles. The most amazing part to me was our ability to complete such a feat in under ten minutes.

We took out the cost for a quarter of a kilo of heroin and divided the rest between us. There was enough left over for us to receive eight thousand apiece. The sum of the take came out to be well over eighty thousand dollars! We never expected to get that amount.

After giving the stolen car a thorough wipe down, we got rid of it, and separated by going our separate ways. We agreed to meet at Fat James apartment to check on his family, and to see if there were any words from him. Of course, I wanted any excuse I could come up with to check in on Destiny. I didn't want to appear as though I was desperate, however, the fact of the matter was, I really was desperate to see her

I walked to my Aunt's house. She only lived a couple of blocks away. When I arrived, Renee greeted me at the door with a warm cheerful hug. She hadn't seen me in quite some time. We spent the entire afternoon catching up. She was no longer singing. Nearly everyone in the group had become heroin addicts, and the group had dissolved.

Renee had begun hanging out with one of the group's former members, named Darlene, and they had befriended some square guys on the northwest side of the city. One of the guys was named Leon. He had just returned from the armed service, and just like most brothers who went to Viet Nam for a tour of duty, he returned to civilian life with a ferocious heroin addiction. These veterans had habits so huge, they seemed insatiable, which is why so many of them overdosed.

Leon turned his best buddy, Maurice, on to this new fad in the black community called snorting Skag. Snorting skag was a technique used to get heroin into your system by inhaling it through your nostrils. Darlene was attracted to Leon's best friend, and because Darlene was trying to get close to him, she loved anything Maurice loved. Renee, like

Leon, were already seasoned users. Getting high together became their favorite recreational activities.

I was devastated to find out my loving, kind, compassionate, cousin had taken on the beast I had just defeated. I began to mourn immediately, because I knew the beast would devour the person she was. Should she ever break the grip of the heroin addiction, she will be different, but for now we had a rare moment, and I intended to take full advantage of it.

Everyone was raving about a new dance craze that was sweeping all the clubs in the city, called the bump. Renee said she could teach me how to do it and turned on the record player. She went through a stack of albums and selected an album by The Ohio Players. She selected the song Fire and put it on. Before the song had played to its' completion, Renee had me Bumping like a pro.

We were having a great time, when her brothers Rodger, and Otis walked in. They stopped in their track upon seeing us, and Otis hollered out, "Awww shit now!" and began dancing with an imaginary dance partner. Rodger joined in by dancing with an imaginary dancing partner of his own. We were feeling the music, and really getting down when Slims' brother Harold let himself in.

"What's up Tone!" he yelled, once he noticed it was me dancing with Renee. "I didn't expect to find you here!" he continued, as he walked towards me. When I stuck out my hand to shake his, he deliberately slapped it out of the way, and hugged me. "Nigga, I've missed you like a mothafucka! What are you doing right now?" When I returned his question with the question, "Why?" he explained to me, he had just gotten a new car, and he was going to this new place everyone was going to shop, called the mall. He invited me to join him, and even offered to buy me a few things if I wanted. I chuckled to myself, because I had over eight thousand dollars in my pocket. He told me Slim went out there and met several of his present hoes. "Man, there's always plenty of rich, white bitches out there, looking for young black men they can pay to spend time with." I guess that was his feeble pitch to make the mall seem even more attractive to me. I agreed to go, but it had nothing to do with his pitch, or his offer. I simply wanted to see for myself what all the fuss was about.

Harold had gotten a Volkswagen Beetle, with a sunroof top. It was also the popular new shade of blue which had been introduced to the public by the major car manufacturers that year. It was a handsome looking car. The snow-white leather interior really complimented the blue exterior.

We left everyone and hopped in his car. On the way to the mall, I told him all about Destiny. Harold and his brothers were my big brothers in every way that mattered. They truly loved me with all their hearts. It was as though I was really their baby brother. He studied me as I spoke of Destiny, and out of concern, he volunteered to give me a ride when I was to meet up with her later that day. He wanted to meet her and felt it would be a great opportunity to do so. I wanted my big brother to see how beautiful Destiny was. I needed confirmation, because I was feeling her far too quickly. I wanted to make sure it wasn't just something I seen. I'd learn over the years that love can blind you.

The mall was amazing. There were at least ten time the amount of shops and stores in the mall, as compared to Downtown. There were statues, and several unique water fountains throughout the interior. The huge plants and trees made you feel like you were inside a beautiful greenhouse. It felt artificial to me, yet it was so beautiful it was stunning. There were lot of large windows everywhere. You felt as though you were outside, the way the sunlight flooded the structure.

Harold took me to get something to eat inside the mall. There was a colorful, well lit, area called the Food Court. Several varieties of fast food restaurants lined the walls. Hamburgers, hot dogs, pizzas, Chinese food and other ethnic cuisine choices were available. There were tables and chairs available for sitting and enjoying the meal you purchased, located in the center of the Food Court.

While we were eating, Harold told me, "I have to tell you something, and it's a secret. I've been working as a makeup artist here." He had taken the training and was now the top sells person in the largest department store in the mall. "Women come from miles away, just for me to do their makeup, and that's how I met my new lady."

He waited to see what my reaction would be. Harold was married to Pandora, so that was his way of informing me of his affair. Pandora was a police cadet in the police academy and was about to graduate. The marriage was rocky to say the least. I got a bad feeling when he told me who his new lady was, and of his plans to leave Pandora, and to move to California with his new lady.

His new lady was none other than, Tisha McKnight! The lead singer of the popular female group, Rapid Relief! I was waiting for the punch line. It wasn't as though Harold wasn't a great catch for any woman, but when someone as close to you as Harold was to me, gets involved with a celebrity, it catches you off guard at first. There wasn't a punch line.

He was quite convincing in his efforts to convince me that this thing he had with Tisha, was more than just an affair. They were so serious he was about to move to California to live with her. He had developed aspirations of becoming a Hollywood makeup artist and expressed his belief of having a better chance at becoming one, if he at least lived in California. He believed he could seek out and take full advantage of opportunities in the movie industry as they arose, if he lived nearby.

After we'd finished our meal, he took me to the chain store he worked. He was the top salesman in the makeup department. All the women were excited to see him and formed a long line to consult with him. He had to do a few makeup jobs, and he amazed me with his skills as an artist. The women were already beautiful, but he made subtle changes and improvements which altered and enhanced their beauty. I was thoroughly impressed.

While he was interacting with the ladies, I noticed for the first time how much he and his brother, Slim, resembled Billy D. Williams. They could all have passed for brothers! With those skills and good looks, the ceiling for his potential was immeasurable.

I felt bad about their marriage. Even though Pandora was about to become a police officer, I was still more than quite fond of her. I loved her. She was always kind and loving towards me, and that meant the world to me. She never treated me like I was anything other than her husband's baby brother.

When Harold first noticed the amount of money I had on me, he was amazed. He looked at me with a look of disappointment and shook his head. I didn't buy much while we were there. I brought a couple of outfits, and convinced Harold to take me to my mom's house to drop them off.

While we were riding to my mother's house, Harold broke the silence. "You're way too smart to end up being just another street nigga Tone!" I braced myself for one of his many lectures. I've never enjoyed getting lectured by anyone, but the sentiment, knowledge, and the wisdom gained was always deeply appreciated, so I listened earnestly as he continued.

"You need to go back to school man. You are the first one out of all of us, to have a real chance to make it out of all this madness. Why do you want to throw it all away?" I had no answer. I was too ashamed to admit I didn't have a clue as to what I should or wanted to do with my life, or what the world could expect from a man like me. Worse yet, after all I'd been through, I still was unexplainably attracted to the life of the streets. It had a pull on me I couldn't seem to resist, break, nor understand.

He was successful at convincing me into at least giving considerable thought to the idea of moving to California with him and getting back in school. Harold had always given me good, sound advice. Slim knew it, and always told me not to listen to that square shit. I was always torn between the two of them, but Harold always made a lot more sense than Slim.

After dropping off my things, we headed to Fat James' apartment a little earlier than planned. This way I could introduce Harold to Destiny, and spend time with her before everyone showed up, and Fat James' trouble became the main topic and the center of everyone's attention.

When Harold saw Destiny, his eyes widened with approval. It was easy to see just how impressed he was with her beauty. To our amazement, Destiny stated right off by saying, she could no longer stomach living in Detroit, and she wanted to move to Los Angeles. She began begging me, right in front of Harold, to go with her.

Harold broke into the conversation and informed her of his plans to move to Los Angeles the following week. He also included that he too was trying to convince me to move to California, so they began double teaming me. Destiny added she had lived there before and knew she could get a job tricking in a massage parlor to support us, until I got back in school.

Harold insisted it wouldn't be necessary for either of us to worry about a place to stay, or anything to eat. "I've got money baby bro. I got you." He studied my face for a clue as to what I was thinking. "We can make it bro!" I promised them I would give it some serious thought and consideration.

At that very moment, Hope walked through the door with June Bug. They were hotly pursued by the remaining members of our crew. They began working on the door as soon as they walked through it. It only took a moment to realize they all were jockeying for Fat James' position in Hopes' life. An opportunity to get with Hope, was the only thing motivating them. Her man, our newest partner hadn't been in jail long at all. It hadn't been twenty-four hours, yet here they were, trying to get with his woman. It dawned on me that although we all claimed to be concerned about Fat James and his family, I was the only one truly concerned.

Someone turned on the record player, and played Earth Wind & Fire's song, Devotion. It made me feel bad to be kicking off a party. It felt inappropriate to be doing anything that felt like a celebration to me. It was obvious we weren't going to discuss any of the issues Fat James' family would have to deal with, so I was ready to leave. Destiny sensed I was becoming upset, so she took my hand, and called out my name.

I wasn't against any of them getting with Hope. I just felt the timing was wrong. He hadn't even appeared before a judge. I told Harold I was ready to go. I gave Destiny a real tight hug. I wanted to make sure she would feel it long after I had gone. I still wasn't comfortable kissing her, though I truly wanted to. I also knew, as soon as I walked through the door, they would be on her as well. I didn't want to appear as though I were as desperate as they appeared to be.

I was far too disappointed in my friend's actions and deeds, to see the obvious. Nothing could have been further from the truth. She would've cherished that first kiss just as much as me. When a woman offers to provide for a man, by using her body, until he gets himself together, it's a pretty fair assumption, she wouldn't object to kissing him.

Suddenly I was overwhelmed with a desire to talk to Marty. I had to tell her all about my plans to move to California. I couldn't get in the car quickly enough. Harold sensed I was having a sucker stroke and broke the silence. "I believe you got mad at your friends for being on Hope the way they were, because you saw yourself in them. None of ya'll owe that nigga shit. You just met this nigga, and never did a single job with him. He hasn't proven himself, the way the rest of ya'll have, with each other. Plus, his woman is fine as a muthafucka! She's just as fine as your woman. A muthafucka gotta be gay as hell to pass on some shit like that! They spouse to be on her ass, just like they were. She gonna like somebody, and be with somebody, so it might as well be one of ya'll. You are tripping!" I thought about what he was saying and laughed out loud. Respect and trust are earned. He was not a member or a true friend. I was tripping. Maybe I was upset because I was just as attracted to Hope as the rest, and I saw myself in my friends, just as Harold had mentioned. I couldn't deny it. Hope was an amazing woman.

Chapter Three

As Harold pulled his car in front of Marty's mother's house, I was more than thrilled by the sight of Marty's latest toy. She had purchased a new, silver Mark four. The Sun roof was opened, which allowed the light from the moon and the streetlight to cascade upon the burgundy interior. It was an instant classic image seared into my memory.

I invited Harold to park his car, so he could come inside to meet Marty. Upon seeing Marty his eyes got just as large as they did when he first saw Destiny. I introduced them to each other, and within the same sentence, I informed him that her husband was Johnny Blue. "The Blues singer?" he asked, unable to conceal the excitement.

"Yes, that's my husband. I call him Johnny B, but this nigga here, is my heart." Then she grabbed me, and began dancing to Berry White's latest hit, Can't Get Enough of Your Love. She was grinding against me so hard, it appeared as though she were riding me.

After the song had ended, she continued squeezing me within her embrace. I detected a slight hint of alcohol, mingled within the aromas of her sweet, expensive perfume. There was no doubt it. She had been drinking, and I can only imagine what else. She was intoxicated and feeling absolutely fabulous! Willie and his friends had a hotly contested Poker game going on at the kitchen table. The activities gave the house a party type atmosphere.

Harold hung out for quite a while. I was so happy he did. I loved my big brothers. He drunk, smoked, ate, laughed, danced and engaged in some deep meaningful conversations. I was thrilled to see just how much he was enjoying himself. We could do this together a lot. After a while I sensed he didn't want to go home. I began to wonder why. It must have been the way I was looking at him that alerted him.

He walked over to me and placed his arm around my shoulders. He pulled me to the side of the room, away from everyone else, and out of their ear shot range, and asked what was really going on between me and Marty. I told him that I wanted her, but she felt I wasn't ready to be in a serious committed relationship yet. He said, "She probably thinks that you will fuck it up right now, and you know what?" He looked at me as we both began laughing, and said in unison, "She's probably right!"

Suddenly his facial expression changed, and so did his mood. He was serious and stressed the need for me to understand the gravity of the situation he was trying to share with me. "I'm going to tell Pandora I want a divorce, tonight. It's time she knew that I'm not happy with our marriage. I really want to move to California to pursue a career in the movie industry as a makeup artist. Whatever you decide to do, going back to school is going to prove to be the best decision you've ever made. Trust me. We're going to do just fine.

He grabbed my right hand in a firm soulful hand shake, while he hugged me with his left arm. "I'll see you tomorrow bro. I had a good time hanging with you today! We need to do a lot more of this." he said as he headed for the door. Marty grabbed me and began dancing to one Stevie Wonder's songs entitled Very Superstitious, just as I was about to walk with Harold to his car. I waved at him as he walked through the door, then I turned my attention towards the task of teaching Marty how to do the bump. We partied all night long.

Marty had begun taking amphetamines, while drinking a Big Mouth Mickey's malt liquor, as her drugs of preference. She was still going strong, when I passed out on the couch next to Tab. Marty was so wired she couldn't sleep if she wanted to.

The next morning as I ventured across the street to my mother's house, I was stopped by Ashley, my mother's next-door neighbor. She waved in a motioning jester indicating she wanted me to come over to her house. She waited patiently on her porch, until I had joined her.

When I looked into her eyes, I could tell something horrible had happened. "What's up?" I asked out of concern. I was hoping that nothing had happened to anyone in her family. Ashly and I were such good friends. We were more like brothers, and sisters. We associated with nearly all the same people, plus she had proven to be one of my biggest fans.

She stared deeply into my eyes, like she was trying to read my mood, before she even spoke a single word. Then she began weeping. "I hate to be the one bringing this shit to you Tone. I swear I do. You don't deserve this bullshit." Then suddenly my whole world was shattered as she spoke the words between sobs. Pandora is in custody. She's being questioned for killing Harold.

The news floored me. I tried to catch myself, but I was unable to. I found myself on the floor of her porch, caught somewhere between the state of disbelief and shock. I instantly became overwhelmed, and grief stricken. It was just far too much for me to absorb. Especially, after spending an entire day with him, and making immediate life changing plans.

I decided to walk straight to Harold's home. He lived only a few blocks from my mother's house. As soon as I reached Buchanan, Slim pulled up alongside me. He stopped his car and yelled, "Get in little brother, Harold's dead!" I was glad he was alone. I had cried while I was walking, and still couldn't stop crying.

After I was settled in the passenger's seat, he attempted to console me, by patting me on my back. I marveled at the unyielding strength Slim displayed. You could see the pain in his eyes, but there wasn't so much as a trace of a tear on his face anywhere, whereas I couldn't stop crying.

He handed me a joint, turned the radio on a jazz station, and merged into traffic. We were headed to Harold's house. Herbie Hancock's song entitled, Tell Me a Bedtime Story, was playing as I lit the joint, and attempted to pass it to Slim. He waved me off and said, "Go ahead lil bro. Smoke on that until you're able to suck it up and pull yourself together. I need you to do just that, before we get there. I don't want those people to detect anything but strength from the both of us.

Those people that he was referring to, were Pandora and her brothers. She was the only girl and she had five brothers. I knew two of her brothers well. Kirkland was much older than the rest of us, and he always offered me words of encouragement. My cousin Rodger worked for her brother Brian, selling heroin. He had a spot in the neighborhood, and Rodger spent most of his time there. When he wasn't working, he spent his leisure time getting high. I loved Brian, just like he truly was a family member, but I didn't like the way he took advantage of Rodger. He paid Rodger a good salary, because he knew Rodger would give him most of the money, if not all the money back getting high on the supply. Rodger loved heroin, and he indulged as often as his money allowed.

When we arrived, Kirkland and Brian came out on the porch to talk to us. Their elderly mother insisted on being there with her daughter, and nothing they could do could convince her to do otherwise. They were concerned that she wasn't truly healthy enough to be in the mix. She did have heart issues, so we all were concerned, but as I said to them, "I love your mom, and you know this, but you can't expect us to leave here without answers. Our brother is dead, and we need to know how that is even possible."

They expected us to be angry, and we were. Slim taught me never to allow anyone to know how I felt about anything, if it were at all possible. As difficult as it was, I was able to contain myself, and listen to their feeble attempts to convince us that their sister was cleaning her service revolver, when it accidently went off, and killed our brother. You couldn't tell by Slims' demeanor If he believed them or not. He was so calm and agreeable, so I followed suit.

We were so cordial and respectful, the brothers invited us into the house to talk to their mother and Pandora. We continued to be polite, respectful, and non-confrontational, as we were warmly received by their apologetic mother. Eventually we were left alone with Pandora. She was also apologetic and looked exhausted as she tried to explain how the accident had occurred. She appeared to be trying her very best to re-collect their last hours together, but she never mentioned anything about a divorce. I couldn't say for certain if Harold had discussed the matter with her or not, but I believed he did. We were forced to depart without further information than we had when we arrived.

As soon as Slim started the car, and pulled out into traffic, I began telling him about everything that was said between me and Harold the day before. I also mentioned, how odd I felt it was for Pandora not to have never mentioned anything about a divorce, in light of what he shared with me in confidence. Slim took a deep breath, and turned to face me, face to face. "Pandora killed Harold. There's no doubt in my mind about it. Everything makes sense to me now. I didn't know about none of this shit!"

We rode to Boulevard Park, one of Harold's favorites locations near the river, and parked. We smoked some weed, drunk some Wild Irish Rose, and listened to some jazz on the radio. I noticed Slim crying for the very first time. "That bitch killed our brother, man!" he managed to say, before we sat in silence for hours with Harold heavy on our hearts.

I broke the silence by telling Slim all about Destiny. He wanted to meet her, so he drove me to the apartment. Destiny was genuinely thrilled to see me and held me within her embrace immediately upon opening the door. When she released me from her arms, I introduced her to Slim. The wound was so huge, and the pain so intense, I couldn't conceal my struggle to utter the words, announcing the death of my brother. I knew if I actually said the words, I would not be able to maintain control of the flood of tears, dammed up inside my soul. So, I stood before her in silence, unable to speak.

"What's wrong Tone?" Destiny asked. Slim recognized

and understood what was going on, so he said the words I was unable to say. I stood there, fighting back tears as Slim explained everything that happened to Destiny. I succeeded in holding back every single tear, and by the time Slim had finished telling her everything, I was able to find my voice.

She told me she understood why I couldn't leave for California at that time. There was just too much going on to depart for new surroundings. It broke my heart not to get to know her more intimately. I wished her well and assured her I would be more than willing to give us a try, if she should ever return.

Then, just as I had done with Harold the night before, I left there heading to see Marty. When we pulled up, everyone was out on the front porch, enjoying the warm evening air and the sunset. We got out of the car, and walked up the sidewalk leading to the house, as everyone stared at us. It was obvious everyone knew by now what had happened. You could sense the concern, and the sympathetic expressions were genuine. As we climb the steps, we were showered with kind words of condolences.

Slim took a seat in the one unoccupied chair, while I took a seat on the bannister. Tab walked up to Slim, and then asked him bluntly, "Are you the pimp?" "Tab!" Marty interrupted with a stern voice, attempting to end the unexpected ambush. It was clear she was embarrassed by her child's sudden interest, and her interrogation of a man grieving the loss of his brother.

Slim assured Marty he wasn't offended by the child's questions. Then he asked Tab how she knew he was a pimp. She was eager to proceed, and answered, "You look just like your brother, who was here last night. I heard my momma say he got killed. I'm sorry. My uncle Derick said his brother was a real pimp, and I believe they're talking about you, because you look like a real pimp."

With a puzzled look on his face Slim asked, "Tell me, just how is a pimp supposed to look, pretty little girl?" She answered without the slightest hesitation, "A cute man, dressed in really nice-looking clothes, with a pocket full of money, and whole lots to say." We all exploded with laughter, and we actually felt the porch sway from our sudden, simultaneous laughter. It was one of those moments in life that images, words, and emotions are captured and seared into memory. Memories which will be summoned during difficult times, to help us make it through.

Slim stayed until nightfall, before he insisted he had to get back to work. "You're the boss bro! Nobody will hold it against you, if you took the day off to mourn our brother." I said in hopes he would stay a little longer. "I wish I could stay here just for you. I know you're hurting just as much as me, but I'm a pimp. A pimp's work is as important as any entertainers, and the same rules apply for us both. No matter what is going on in our lives, the show must go on. I have hoes just waiting to catch me slipping, just so they can attempt to give me grief. I have clients, with mental health issues, and their wellbeing depends entirely upon the services we provide. We prevent eccentric people from committing rapes, murder, and in some cases, mass murders. All sort of deviant behavior, including adultery, are curtailed simply because of the services my ladies provide. Ladies who depend on me for protection and guidance. I'm sorry little brother, but I must leave." Before he hugged me and left, he made me give my word I would not to go on sociopathic, violent rampage. I assured him I would be fine and watched as he walked to his car.

Marty hovered over me the entire time I was there, making sure my glass was never empty of gin and lime juice. We both were hoping I would get drunk and pass out, but it wasn't working. I was in too much pain to feel the effects of any form of intoxicants. I thought getting high and spending time with Marty would ease the pain, but that also wasn't working, so I walked to the Hole in the Wall bar.

When I arrived, I found June Bug and JB were already there looking for me. They had heard about Harold, and like Slim, they were concerned about me, and my violent temper. They were also ready to purchase our sack and needed another five thousand dollars from me. They had made a deal to get another quarter of pure, uncut, heroin for twenty-five thousand. That would be my share of the cost. It would be strong enough for us to cut into three and a half kilos, and still be too strong for sells on the streets.

I gave JB five thousand dollars and watched as he added it to the rest of the money he had in a leather, money belt, which he wore under his clothing. He and June Bug left together, while I waited at the bar. June Bug was driving, and these were JB's people.

Even back then, we didn't want to ride with too many young black men in a car. That was the quickest way to get pulled over by the police. Nowadays they call it, Driving While Black. There was no name for it back then, but it was strictly enforced. The larger the number of young black men in a car, the higher the probability of getting harassed by the police. Being a young black man in America teaches you, you must learn how to play the percentages, if you're to survive.

I sat at the bar and had a catching up conversation with my dear friend Kari. She was the new bar tender, and she really knew her trade. She made me a Victor Alexander, and while we sat there talking she used the neck of a beer bottle to demonstrate the techniques she use to stroke a penis. It was so distracting, I had to leave the bar to get some fresh air, and to regain some semblance of control.

I stepped outside the bar, and as I did so, I fired up a joint. My mind was on Kari, and I wasn't paying any attention to my surroundings. When I looked to my right, I noticed the squad car for the very first time. The Officers who occupied the vehicle were looking directly at me when I lit the joint, so I spun on my heels and re-entered the bar.

Upon entering the bar, I immediately threw the joint to the un-kept floor and crushed it beneath the sole of my shoe. I used my foot to spread it around, to make it even more difficult to detect. I then put as much distance between me and the evidence as possible, by walking briskly to the rear of the establishment. As soon as I had made it to the rear, the officers walked through the front door.

They were looking for me, and just as I thought, I was their soul focus. As soon as eye contact was made, it was a done deal. They walked right over the evidence, as though they truly were in hot pursuit of a dangerous felon.

After obtaining my identification one of the officers searched the floor near my feet with a flashlight. The other officer kept engaging me with pointless questions. They couldn't find anything on the floor, so they ran my information for outstanding warrants. All the while I wasn't worried at all. I knew there were no warrants, so my attitude was a little boastful. You can't imagine the horror I felt in my gut as one of the officers informed me of my rights! There was a warrant for my arrest out of Hudsonville for simple assault. I was taken into custody, and immediately transported to the city jail.

The Sheriff's deputies arrived early the next morning and transported me to the county jail in Grand Haven. It had been a long night, considering I had just handed most of my money to JB. I barely got any sleep at all. An assault charge, I thought had been dismissed while I was attending State University, had been brought back up. To avoid facing prison time, I pled guilty to simple assault, which carried a maximum penalty of ninety days in jail, and/ or a hundred dollar fine. The judge sentenced me to the maximum of ninety days with a sixty-day review date to be considered for early release.

I remembered the incident quite well and could not believe I was doing time for cussing out a student who had a job of passing out special activities' equipment. On that day some black students had a spades card game going on in the dorm lobby. I was so bored, I walked over to the table to see what type of skills they had and compare them to my own. I was thinking about joining them.

One of the girls playing was Alicia. She was a very pretty black girl, but she battled with a weight problem. Even though she was considered obese by medical standards I loved her body. She had a very curvy body without a trace of cellulite. Her provocative walk, and a huge shapely buttock, demanded the attention which it undoubtedly received whenever she walked across a crowded room.

On more than one occasion she had sought my attention and succeeded in convincing me to sneak to her room. We had to sneak, but she didn't mind. She knew I didn't want Toni to find out. Toni would not have cared about me having another woman. The truth was, I didn't want to be in a relationship with Alicia.

We would listen to jazz, smoke weed, kiss and bump grind until she could not take it any longer. She then would nearly rip my pants open to release my penis, before nearly swallowing my entire shaft without gaging. Oral sex was frowned upon in the black community back in those days among the squares who had no idea what it was they were missing. She obviously loved, and mastered the art of fellatio, and it was more than my pleasure to keep her little secret.

She also had two huge older brothers that played on the school's football team. I was the starting strong safety, and they were both starting on the defensive line, so we were teammates. I didn't want the sex I was having with their baby sister, without being in a relationship, to complicate things between us.

I watched as Alicia took a sip from what appeared to be a milkshake and sat it down on the table beside her. I picked up her cup and took a sip. Considering the secret of hers I kept, I believed it to be okay, but she exploded. "You muthtafucka! You can gone ahead and keep it now! I'm not drinking behind you, you nasty mouth muthafucka!"

Everyone in attendance burst into a gut bursting laughter. I was shocked, hurt and embarrassed by her outburst. I stood there looking at the many different faces of the people looking directly into my face and laughing at me. I couldn't stand for being treated so rudely in front of a crowd of people by someone I was intimate with. Not without retaliation that is. I took the top off the milkshake and poured the remaining contents all over the top of her head and threw the empty cup to the floor.

Once again, everyone burst into laughter. This time the eyes were focused on her, as the tall full afro hairdo she wore was flattened by the weight of the thick, dark liquid. The syrupy chocolate milkshake ran like a water fountain, from the top of her head to her face. "I'm gonna call my brothers, and get your ass whipped! That's what the fuck I'm gonna do!" were the last words she mumbled as she humbly, but hurriedly ran from the lobby.

I knew exactly what I was up against, so I immediately ran to the equipment counter, and threw my student identification card on the counter, and ordered a baseball bat. The student working behind the counter refused to give me the bat, so I hopped over the counter and got the bat myself. When the student approached me, demanding the bat, I raised it in a threatening manner and warned him, "Get out of my way, before I fuck yo bitch ass up." Once he was out of my way, I proceeded to the lobby's entrance.

I stood by the door, with the bat clutched in my hands, and ready to fight. I was determined not to run, nor lose in the confrontation, no matter what the odds were. When the brothers arrived, they found me armed with a bat, so they were beyond reluctant to bum rush me. No matter what they did, one of them was bound to get seriously injured by the bat I was yielding. They weren't going away. They separated, and one got in front of me, while the other got behind me. They waited for an opening or a blind side to take advantage of. They wanted to make an attempt at taking the bat away from me.

At that very moment Gator, Box, Meme, and some huge

light skinned guy with muscles literally everywhere, came through the door. The light skinned guy with all the muscles also had a face full of freckles. He asked Gator, "Is that Tone?" Gator answered, "Yeah man! That's him. In trouble, as usual."

He and Gator came and stood beside me. Gator suggested that I put the bat down. It wasn't really a suggestion, and just that quickly, I had been convinced the bat wouldn't really be necessary at all. The big guy spoke directly to the brothers, "You fellas have a problem with our youngster?" He said it in a way to make sure emphasis was placed on the word, "...our...".

The brothers didn't want to fight all five of us, so they agreed to drop everything, if I would give my word to apologize to their sister, which I readily agreed to do. I felt horrible about my act of retaliation. It was the very first time I had been in her presence, and it wasn't a pleasurable experience. I had planned on finding out what the whole incident was about, and how it went so horribly wrong. I was willing to do whatever it was that was necessary to make things right between us again, for obvious reasons.

After they had gone, Gator introduced me to the guy with the muscles and the freckles. This is Day Day, the dude I've been telling you all about. I was thrilled to meet him. Not only because he had just saved my ass, but because I was thoroughly impressed by every single story I had ever heard about him. Now, I had actually witnessed him in action. He was considered a legend in the state's prison system.

The next day I was arrested by the county sheriff department, for threating the student behind the counter with the baseball bat, and I ended up spending the night in jail. The following morning, I was told the case had been dropped, and I was free to go. Now, here I was in the county jail, serving a ninety-day sentence.

None of this could have happened at a worse time. It meant I would miss Destiny's departure for California. I had just invested thousands on a business venture with nothing but a handshake, and now I'm going to be missing for at least sixty days. I could handle all of these things, but there was no way I could easily handle not being allowed to attend Harold's funeral. To qualify to attend his funeral, I had to prove he was a member of my immediate family. That wasn't possible.

After spending a couple of weeks in the pods with the general population, a deputy came to escort me to Sheriff Neblett's office. Upon entering his office, the first thing I noticed was how beautiful the wood was, and there was a lot of it. He was talking on the phone, while sitting in a tall back, brown leather, swivel chair. The huge mahogany desk was a magnificent piece of art itself.

He made a gesture indicating he wanted the deputy to leave us alone, and the deputy promptly made his exit. He ended his phone conversation, and offered me a cigarette after lighting one for himself. Whenever a member of law enforcement offers a cigarette to someone in custody, there are ulterior motives at play. They are trying to get you to relax you, so they can pump as much information out of you as they possibly can. They are not trying to be nice just because they're nice guys. They warn you that anything you say, can and will, be used against you. Afterwards they depend on you getting comfortable and careless.

He offered me a position on the trustee staff. My duties would include taking out all the garbage, passing out all the meals in general population, cutting hair during intake, and washing the squad cars. I would have full days, but there were plenty of benefits to staying busy in jail. It always seems to help the time go by smoother and faster. There were other benefits also. We ate as much as we wanted or whatever we felt like cooking, if we didn't want to eat the meal prepared by the cook, Mrs. Neblett, the sheriff's wife.

The trustees were housed in a dorm, which was never locked. There was a telephone we could use any time we wanted to use it. The only problem there was to placing a call, you could only make collect calls. There was a television, a radio, and free-weights for us to workout with whenever we had a spare moment. I knew I would be working out a lot. I accepted the position and rose to be led to the trustee's living quarter, when the sheriff asked me to remain seated, because we had further business to discuss.

He went on to explained how seriously out of control the drug problem had gotten on campus. They were so desperate now he was willing to think outside the box for a solution. He asked me to pose as a drug dealer and collect as much information as I possibly could while undercover. I would report directly to him, and only to him. In return they would purchase a fancy expensive car, and the clothes needed for me to successfully play the part. My tuition, and room and board, would be taken care of. I would also receive a weekly salary of one thousand dollars for as long as I worked for them.

He didn't want an answer right then. He gave me his card and had one of his cards placed in my property. He told me because I was a trustee, I was guaranteed to be released after sixty days. "Think about it for about a month after you're released. Discuss it with your family." He concluded his presentation by adding, should I decide to accept the offer, all I had to do was call him. In the meantime, I could smoke cigarettes, eat all I wanted to eat, and enjoy the comforts of living in the trustee dorm.

I remembered Unck's phone number, so I tried to call him collect to see if he would accept the charges. I was extremely happy, when he not only accepted the charges, but also was thrilled to hear from me. He was even a little upset that I had not called sooner. He was very happy to inform me that June Bug, and JB were raking in the cash after I informed him I had an invested interest. I felt relieved, because that meant my investment was safe.

I used the phone book to look up Ms. Melissa Walters. I called her collect, and to my surprise she accepted the charges. She was very happy to hear from me. She even made the trip to come visit me. It shocked me to see how much weight she had lost. She told me, she and Coach were no longer in contact with one another. She said the last thing she heard about him, was when he got a head coaching job at some high school. "I'm not trying to contact that horrible man. That ship sailed a long, long time ago. That was the last time I ever saw Melissa.

Being a trustee did make the time seem to pass quickly. All I did with my spare time, was eat and workout with the free-weights. I had gotten huge, and more than ready to throw my weight around. Before I knew it, I was on a Greyhound bus, schedule to arrive in Newport at nine in the morning. I really was looking forward to getting my share of our investment. I had been gone for two months. Even though I had absolutely no idea of how much I should expect, I knew I had a lot of money coming.

I used a dime at a pay phone to call my brother, who

promptly came to pick me up at the bus station. When he arrived, he had a joint already rolled, and was filled with joy. I was his big brother, and we shared a bond that will never be understood by an outsider.

He was excited because he had started a new business venture himself. He was selling nickel and dime bags, and the weed was excellent! We smoked some of it, as we rode home. He took full advantage of the time he had alone to fill me in on everything that had been going on in the family while I was away. He took me straight to momma's house and dropped me off. He made a few promises to hook up with me late in the day.

Before I could get out of the car good, I heard a woman's voice pierce the stillness of the morning. "What type of bird don't fly?" she asked. It was Marty! She was smiling, jumping up and down, and waving. I ran across the street, as she ran down the stairs. We met on the sidewalk in front of her mother's house.

Either no one was out that morning, or we were so into each other nether one of us would have noticed if there were. She jumped into my arms, and wrapped her legs around my waist, and slid her sweet tasting tongue into my mouth.

It felt great to have the love of my life in my arms once again, after so many lonely nights spent thinking of her, longing for her, and as usual she was once again making my dreams come true. As always, she never asked what happened. She has always been thrilled just to have me home and relished in the moment we had the opportunity to share.

Chapter Four

Albert told me he had informed June Bug I would be home at nine o'clock in the morning. After hanging out with Marty for a few hours, and not hearing from any of my friends, I became extremely upset. Marty tried unsuccessfully to get me to calm down. Their failure to meet with me and welcome me home, was as much of an insult as a slap in the face, as far as I was concerned. I struck out on foot seeking them out. I was disappointed, but unbeknown to me, my disappointments were just beginning and about to pile up.

After checking at several of bars in the neighborhood within walking distance, I ran into JB in the Bucket of Blood. He smiled nervously as he greeted me. He found it difficult to conceal his nervousness as he switched from side to side in his seat. He was avoiding eye contact with me and was quite evasive in his answers to my questions. Eventually he suggested we go to the spot. "June Bug is there, and he'll explain everything. Come on. I can take you to him in the car right now."

I instantly knew I was about to receive some unsettling news. Why else would he need June Bug to explain things to me. Whatever it was June Bug was about to explain to me, JB didn't have the courage to do so. I felt like I was caught in the twilight zone. I could feel it in my gut. Something wasn't right about my comrades. I felt I was about to be double crossed.

When we pulled up in front of a clean nice looking house in the middle of the block, I was surprised when JB told me this was the spot. There were a few people mulling around in front of the house, whom I recognized. They were heroin addicts I had served before. They all seemed to light up, once they recognized JB's car. They were ready to test his heart for a soft spot, which might reward its' finder with anything from some pocket changes to a free hit.

As we exited the car, a couple of the fellas recognized me, and rushed over to the car to greet me. They were acting as though I was a celebrity, but that is how most guys who return to the neighborhood are treated after a term of incarceration.

Walking through the doors of the house, was like walking into another world. Everything in the house was filthy, and that included the floors, the walls, and the kitchen. You could smell the stench of urine coming from the bathroom, therefore actually seeing its' condition wasn't necessary. All of this was an unbelievable contrast in comparison to the outwardly appearance of the house.

People were lined up from the front door, all the way to the kitchen table, waiting to be served by June Bug. There was a couple of young guys carrying baseball bats, barking orders to those in the line. It kept things orderly and running smoothly. June Bug sat at the kitchen table serving everyone and raking in the dough. Upon seeing me, I noticed he too flashed the same nervous smile as JB did earlier.

"Hey bro!" he said as he rose to his feet. He vigorously shook my right hand as he embraced me with he left arm. "Welcome home boy!" he said just before turning to one of the youngsters keeping the line in order and ordered him to take over. He then led me and JB to an empty room. We had some business to discuss, and we needed privacy to resolve our serious and sensitive issues.

As we entered the empty room, the first thing I noticed was it was the cleanest room in the house. Even though there was dust everywhere, there was no clutter. "Things aren't as they appear to be." were June Bugs first words.

I responded by stating, "If you're talking business wise, things look pretty damn good to me!" He continued by explaining how the business he, JB, and I had put together, had gotten raided. He said we lost everything, because they had to flush it all down the toilet to prevent getting caught with it. After that, he claimed he and JB put their money together and started a new business; this business.

You never know how strong you are until a situation challenges you. I had to contain myself and conceal my anger. This would not be my day of retribution. It appeared to be nothing I could do except accept it, but I knew I would not be denied what I believed was rightfully mine; only delayed. I was going to retaliate, but not at that very moment, under their roof.

I hid my disappointment. My best friends had crossed me once again. I say once again because, they had excluded me before, when they robbed Dayton's sister. The take was considerably larger than any of the robberies we had committed up to that time. I unintentionally led Dayton directly to their hideout. They were in the process of splitting up the loot between them, when we walked in on their secret gathering.

There I stood. Stunned beyond belief. They each gave

me one hundred dollars apiece as a welcoming home jester. I physically accepted the offering, but not in my heart. They would pay dearly for underestimating the consequences of taking money from me. It was just a matter of being patient.

While smiling I announced, "Well, I'm not spending any money here, so I better find something to do. Can't hang out here watching ya'll getten money. Just ain't never been my style. I'm glad to see things working out for ya'll. You know how to reach me, should you need me." I held my head high, and walked with plenty of pip in my step, as I walked towards the door. I proceeded to act as though I was on top of the world, even though I had just lost thousands.

I decided to walk to my brother's house. He lived about a quarter of a mile from where I was located. The walk would give me some time to think. I wasn't going for that lame ass play they had tried to pull on me, but this was a very delicate situation. I would have to give this a lot of thought. I had been robbed, and I fully intended to return the favor in kind.

When I arrived at my brother's house, I was surprised to find my good friend Joe Thomas had come to town and was waiting for me. We smoked some weed and reminisced about our high school days. He caught me up on all the latest developments in Tri City. He also informed me the child that wasn't supposed to be mine, was beginning to look more and more like me every day. It confirmed my suspicions. I had a daughter in Tri City, and that much was for sure as far as I was concerned.

We eventually left my brother's house. I wanted to see Marty and spend the remainder of the day celebrating my return to the free world. Marty's mom cooked fried chicken, green beans, mashed potatoes with brown gravy, and homemade biscuits. She claimed she did it just for me. Biggum was known as an excellent cook, and the meal was only a sample of her culinary skills. I hadn't had a real home cooked meal in months. I devoured the meal while trying not to appear famished. Both Marty and Biggum were very pleased to see me enjoying the food. She knew there was a strong possibility I would stay in for the remainder of the night, and that pleased them both.

Afterwards I sipped on some Tanqueray gin and lime juice, while puffing on some Columbian red bud. I placed my head on Marty's lap, and listened to The Isley Brothers latest album. She gently massaged my temples, while kissing me all over my face. The last thing I remembered as I began to drift off to sleep, was Marty whispering in my ear. "Baby, whatever it is that has you so worked up, it too will soon pass. I promise you." She said it as though it was such a matter of fact, I became thoroughly convinced of it myself. That's all it took for me to truly believe her. She was my biggest fan, and if she said I could do something, you could bet your last dollar I could.

I never told Marty I was upset. Somehow, she knew. I know I had done a masterful job of concealing my anger, but there was no way I could hide anything from her. She could feel me. If I was in a joyful mood, she knew it. If my heart was heavy with grief, she knew it. If I turned down food being offered to me, because I was trying to be polite, she would insist that I ate. To make sure I ate, Marty would always fix a plate for me, and place it inside her mother's oven. That was regardless of what my answer was. If I felt overwhelmed with worry, she knew it, without me so much as uttering a single word. She unexplainably knew and understood me. Sometimes I believe no one else ever will.

Joe stayed up all night playing poker with Willie and his friends and made out like a bandit. He won over three hundred dollars. When I woke up, I told Joe all about how June Bug and JB had played me. It was painful and difficult, but I explained to Joe how the friends I had so proudly bragged to him about had now become my adversaries.

Joe heard all about Slim years ago, and the effect the man had on my life. He longed to meet him, so I surprised him with my plans to find Slim and hang out with him for a few days. As I observed his reaction, I realized he felt the same way as I did my first time meeting Slim. When I chuckled, Joe asked me what was funny. I answered, "Nothing" as I noticed the opportunity to take advantage of the empty bathroom and made a mad dash for it. Most houses were built with only one bathroom in the home, so if you needed to use the rest room, you couldn't take for granted it would be unoccupied once you were ready to use it.

I called the only number I had to contact Slim, and to my surprise he answered the phone himself. I found it unusual for him to answer, because one of his hoes would always be assigned with the secretarial duties. He was as excited as I was about the opportunity to spend a few days with each other. He knew exactly where Marty lived, and insisted upon picking me up. During the beginning of the conversation, I warned him that I had Joe with me, but he assured me it wasn't a problem.

It wasn't long before Slim was in front of the house, blowing his horn. The Cadillac had a unique sound back in those days. It was unlike any other make or model. I recognized the horn, so I immediately instructed Joe to get ready to leave, but to wait until I'd said my goodbyes. I thanked Biggum for the hospitality and passed out kisses to show my appreciation. Of course, Marty was the only one to taste my tongue.

As we rode through the traffic, I told Slim the whole story of how and when I had gotten played. He listened to me attentively and waited until I had finished before responding. "I wanted to hang out with you for a couple of days, but it won't be long before word gets out on the streets that they played you like a lame ass bitch. You must retaliate. You must deliver a severe enough blow, to inflict the maximum amount of damage. You must leave no doubt that you've been amply compensated, and you've snatched your desired justice from the muthafuckas who attempted to deny you."

"What must I do? How is it possible to make such a masterful move? All I have is myself." Slim changed the subject, so in response I fell silent. When we entered his apartment the seven hoes he had in his stable, all scrambled to find some space on the floor, in front of a chair. They kneeled before the chair in a praying position. I remember thinking they were worshipping a chair! No one will ever truly understand the shock I experienced as I watched Slim climb upon the chair and stretch out his arms as though he were presenting himself. My brother was mocking religion and using it as a tool. The hoes were praying to him in unison. "Dear Almighty Hand, I thank you for choosing to return to us. Without you I am but a lost sheep, and fair game for all predators. With your guidance and protection, I am no longer an endangered species, but I've become a predator as well. Though I work through the darkness of night, I will fear no evil, for I know your almighty hands will forever guide, comfort and protects me. Amen."

Joe and I both turned to face each other. Never had either of us ever heard of such control, let alone witnessed it. It gave us the feeling we had just witnessed a rare event unlike any we will ever experience in life again. Our facial expressions told the entire story. We both were completely astonished and impressed to say the least.

We stayed up most of the night listening to Slim explain how he had incorporated theology into the pimp game. It was quite simple. All he did was inserted himself into the position of the deity being worshiped. Other times he would insert himself into the role of the prophet. He studied the bible and knew it by heart. Not to lead sheep to salvation, but to lead them all astray. It just seemed like there was something inherently wrong with tampering with theology.

Eventually Joe became exhausted by the day's activities and needed some rest. Slim put him in a bedroom with two of his hoes and closed the door. I didn't know it at the time, but he had given strict instructions to keep Joe so occupied and entertained, he couldn't have cared less about what was going on outside of that room.

The very first thing Slim asked me once we were comfortable in our seats in his living-room was, "Are you sure your man is ready, and has the heart to get involved in the affairs of gangsters?" I was honest in my response to his question. "I can't say for sure he is ready or not, but he's convinced me he has the heart." He took out a spanking brand new nine-millimeter pistol and handed it to me. The excitement I felt was so uncontainable, I had to be reminded we were trying not to disturb the threesome in the bedroom.

The last thing Slim said before showing me where I could sleep was, "Test Joe, before taking him on any jobs, or as a partner. I may be wrong, but your boy looks like a trembler to me." A trembler is a guy who freezes and trembles with fear in the face of danger when action is necessary.

That next night we spent some time at Lou's bar with. I wanted Joe to get a real feel for the streets, among true street players. I sat at the bar, and from where I sat I could easily observe the cars that rode pass. I paid even closer attention to the cars that parked. Its' occupants were going either to the store next door or coming inside the bar.

As I sat there staring out the window, I noticed JB pull up to the curb. When he hopped out of the car, I noticed he was as sharply dressed as I had ever seen him. That was a great indication he was experiencing some degree of prosperity. After entering the bar, he nodded his head in my direction to acknowledge me and headed to the opposite end of the bar. Although the bar was packed, there were plenty of open seats available near me. He elected not to sit near me by choice. He also avoided eye contact, which told me something or someone was making him very uncomfortable.

I walked over to him to see if I could get a better understanding of this look I'd never noticed in his eyes before. I made up a story about wanting to get with a chick. I told him I hadn't had a woman since I'd been released from jail. The way I explained it to him, the girl I had in mind was a heroin addict and if I was able to provide her with enough drugs, she would allow me to do whatever I wanted to her.

"You know I feel fucked up about the way all of this shit turned out. You're my man Tone. I'll tell you what. I don't have anything right now, because we are getting ready to reup, but as soon as we reup I'm going to give you a whole spoon uncut. That'll be enough to lay up with several of those dope-fiend hoes!" He exploded into laughter from his gut, while studying my reaction. I had to get a little animated, but I was able to convince him that we shared the same opinion of hoes.

He told me he was waiting on his girl, so she could ride with him, because he didn't want to look too conspicuous. If a young black man rode alone in a late model car, he was just as likely to get stopped and harassed by the police, as a car full of young black males. You had a much better chance of not being harassed if you appeared to be on a date. He ordered a beer, and I took a walk back to the other end of the bar. As I was returning to my seat, I got a brilliant idea. I knew exactly what I was going to do to get the retribution I deserved.

I returned to my seat near the entrance but at the other end of the bar. From the vantage point I was seated, I was able to look out the huge picture window and observe all three street corners. I continued to pay closer attention to the cars that parked near the front of the bar. Every car that drove pass the bar, in either direction had my attention. I had to make sure JB was alone before putting my master plan into motion. The plan had to work before his lady friend showed up.

Francine was a high yellow, older, obese woman with the most perfectly shaped buttock anyone had ever seen. She was working behind the bar. She was much older than me but had expressed on many occasions her desire to have sex with me.

One night I overheard her confiding with someone about her man problems. She was interested in a fella, but he wasn't interested in her. She had tried her very best to seduce him but couldn't figure out why nothing ever worked. I knew the guy she was talking about, and knew he had an amazingly beautiful wife.

Later that very night I had a talk with Francine and took full advantage of the information and opportunity to convince her I was able to see things just by looking at the palms of her hands. I explained to her how the Universe had guided me to her with a message. I also informed her of how badly I wanted to see what she could do with all that ass. It was too much ass for most men, but I wasn't most men.

I proceeded to hold her hand in mine face up and pretended to read her situation based upon the lines on her hand. I warned her of a man I seen she wanted but couldn't seem to throw the ass at. "The man is happily married, and that's the only reason he doesn't want to fuck that big fine yellow ass of yours, but I do. When you find out for sure the man is married, get back with me, and reward me!"

Less than a week later she found out for sure about the man's wife and was determined to have me from that point on. She even claimed I was her man to several patrons who frequent the bar. She believed I was a prophet sent specifically for her, and now here she was exactly where I needed her to be.

I got her attention, which was never hard for me to do, and signaled with my index finger for her to come to me. She hurriedly walked in my direction, switching her buttocks as hard as she could. I knew if I promised her the night of her life, she would comply with my request, without hesitation.

I promised her we would get together that very night if she did me a huge favor. Joe had a puzzled look on his face and so did she. They knew I was up to something and it was much deeper than what appeared as the obvious on the surface. They didn't have a clue as to what it was. Joe watched me attentively as I handed Francine a twenty-dollar bill and instructed her to flirt with JB. "Make sure he drinks as much beer as he possibly can in as short of time as possible." She smiled, licked her lips, and blew a kiss in my direction. She then balled up my twenty-dollar bill and tossed it on the bar in front of me. She proceeded to do precisely as I had instructed her to do to the letter. JB was so mesmerized by the thought of possibilly playing with her huge ass, he never noticed me getting up and moving. I sat at a table near the men's restroom.

Joe was watching my every move. I knew JB would have to use the restroom soon to relieve himself. He continuing to consume large amounts of beer. There was a pool table near the men's restroom, so I pretend to be deeply engrossed in the game being played.

Francine turned around while rubbing her big ass and was smiling at JB over her shoulder. When he finally rose to his feet he stumbled a bit, but he was able to regain his balance by using his hands to catch the edge of the bar. He then continued towards the rest room. I watched as he entered the restroom and by using my mind, I imagined I were in the restroom with him watching his every move. I knew Francine's flirting and the effects of the beer would place him in a totally confident, relaxed and peaceful state of mind. I timed it perfectly. I could hear the strong flow of his urine hitting the water, as I quietly entered the restroom.

Before he realized I had also entered the restroom, I had the barrel of my pistol pressed firmly to the temple of his head. Joe entered the restroom shortly afterwards and held the door open a little too long. I barked for him to close the door, and to come immediately to my aid.

Joe went through all of his pockets as I instructed and found approximately two thousand dollars. "This is fucked up, what you're doing Tone!" JB protested. He had no idea how badly things were about to get. We were once partners, and he was trying to pull a fast one on me at that very moment.

"Shut the fuck up muthafucka. I don't want to hear a muthafucken thing you got to say. Now lift your shirt up, so I can get to that fucken money belt. That's what the fuck you can do." Then I pressed the pistol a little harder against his head to put emphasis on my last words. JB knew me very well. Well enough to know I wasn't playing and if he wanted to live, he shouldn't try me.

"Tone are you seriously robbing me?" he asked, as though he were in a state of shock and total disbelief. When he lifted his shirt, I snatched the Velcro money belt from around his waist myself.

"I promise you I will kill you, if you come out of this bathroom." I then ordered him to have a seat in the stall and exited the restroom behind Joe. I stopped at the bar, just for a moment, to inform Francine I would be calling the bar to tell her where to meet me. I motioned my head towards the door as a signal for Joe to follow me. Fortunately, I was able to hail a cab, and immediately headed to my brother's house.

The very first thing I did upon arriving at my brother's house, was call the bar. She answered the phone laughing. Once she had gathered herself and realized it was me on the line, she gave me a summation of what occurred after I left. JB told her they would have to catch up to each other some other time.

She added that he was clearly shaken, and just as I had expected, his lady friend arrived just moments before June Bug. She then gave me the address to her apartment, and I in return I gave her my brother's phone number. I instructed her to call me at that number once she arrived home, and I would catch a cab there.

I had a sum of sixteen thousand dollars. There was only two thousand in twenty-dollar bills. The rest of the money was all fifty and hundred-dollar bills. It was a pretty impressive bank roll, to say the least. When we were in business together, we used to travel from bank to bank and from store to store, seeking opportunities to trade in the five, ten and twenty-dollar bills in for fifties and hundreds. I was sure that was exactly what JB and June Bug had done. I gave Joe five hundred dollars just for being with me when everything went down. After Francine called, I gave my brother fifty dollars for some weed and a ride to her apartment.

Chapter Five

Francine answered the door in a red see-through full-length flowing nightgown with nothing underneath it. Although she was fully covered, there was nothing left for the imagination. It was quite obvious what she had on her mind, as well as what she expected. She was an amazing sight, and the fragrance from the burning incense and her perfumes were intoxicating. Together they were much more than stimulating. There was something awaking inside of me. I had a taste for the exotic, and it appeared to be exactly what I was about to get. She was so sexy! Fulfilling my end of the bargain wasn't going to be a difficult task at all.

I took her in my arms and kissed her hard and deeply for a long time. Big girls love to be treated as though they are small, and there was no procrastination in my game. I swept her off her feet in my arms and carried her through her immaculate apartment to the sofa. I only told her once before how much I enjoyed jazz, and she remembered. My favorite Freddie Hubbard tune, First Light, was playing. I don't know if she knew it was my favorite, but it was playing. The only light throughout the entire apartment, was a red light illuminating from her bedroom, a short distance down a corridor.

While we were on the sofa, I was kissing, hugging, and rubbing her all over. There was just so much of her for me to enjoy, I couldn't make up my mind where I wanted to linger. After a while, I stopped for a moment. It seemed like I had been kissing, licking ass and sucking tits for about an hour, but actually it had only been twenty minutes.

My finger eventually found her clit and was instantly moisten by the flow of fluids from her vagina. I twirled my finger in small imaginary circles around her clit to the sounds of her groans and moans. She unzipped my pants and freed my erect penis. She stroked it ever so carefully, trying her best to make it maintain a firm stiff erection, while at the same time she was trying to take me right to the threshold of ejaculation, without actually making me explode. It was a delicate balancing act to perform, but a task she handled magnificently.

Freddie Hubbard's tune entitled Red Clay begun playing when I once again attempted to pick her up. She protested slightly, "Baby, I can walk. You're gonna hurt yourself." Of course, I knew it was both a challenge and a test. After I swooped her up, all you could hear from her were giddy giggles of delight. She couldn't believe she was being carried, yet she was on her way to the bedroom without using any of her own energy.

The bedroom was done in pink, and white. The solid oak bed had a canopy made up with some sheer white material draped over it, and it wrapped all the way around the bed. All the walls were painted pink and the base boards, door and window trimmings were all done in white. While still holding her in my arms, I placed one of my knees on the bed for leverage, to be assured of laying her down gently. I took off my money belt and place it on the night stand. Then I took the weed out of my pocket.

"Oh goodie! You have weed!" she gleefully chirped, as she hopped out of the bed and landed on her feet. "I have the perfect wine for us." She then disappeared into the darkness to retrieve this so-called perfect wine.

While she was busy preparing the wine, I took the liberty in her absence to roll a few joints. Shortly after I started rolling the last of three joints, she arrived carrying a bucket of ice, with a bottle of Manischewitz Blackberry wine chilling in it. In her other hand, she was toting two wine glasses.

She sat the wine glasses on her night stand. I watched as she poured the dark liquid into the glasses. She picked up one of the glasses and handed it to me. She waited until I had taken a sip, all the while she was searching my face for some sort of sign of approval. The wine was sweet and taste like berries. I had not yet developed a true palate for wine, so I was impressed by the dark sweet drink. I gave her my nod as a sign of approval and lit up one of the joints. She smiled while looking towards the floor blushing.

After taking just one good toke, I was beginning to feel the mellow effect of the wine and marijuana. I was thinking of how good my brother's weed was as I passed her the joint. She put the joint between her lips, and took a long deep draw. Thereby inhaling the smoke deeply into her lungs. I stood up and removed every stitch of clothing I had on and laid back down across the bed.

Once we had finished smoking, we began kissing again. I lightly kissed and nibbled upon her neck and shoulders. She smelled so strong of perfume, I could almost swear she took a bath in it. The smell was too strong, yet the scent was sweet. I felt compelled to tough it out. My erect penis was proof it wasn't a deal breaker. All the times in the past she had wanted me, but now the tables were reversed. I wanted her.

As I kissed on her neck I twisted one of her nipples between my thumb and fore finger. I kept it up until it stood swollen and stiff. I lowered my face and got a firm lip lock on her thick swollen nipple. A nursing infant could not have given her nipple more attention than I did at that very moment. I wanted to continue sucking on the sweet stiff nipple, but after a while my instincts kicked in and warned me of the envy building up inside the left breast. Of course, I didn't want that, so I switched to the left nipple and showed it an equal amount of attention.

"Baby will you please eat my pussy?" she begged me, as she squirmed and rubbed her vagina. She stared deeply into my eyes searching for and anticipating an answer. I never responded verbally. Instead of answering her with words, I rolled her over on her stomach and squeezed the cheeks of her buttocks in my huge hands. I pulled her cheeks apart thereby exposing her anus. Oh, what a lovely sight it was. You had to be a serious fan of a woman's anatomy, to fully appreciate what I had lying before me.

I stuck my thumb in my mouth for a brief moment, to moisten it with my saliva. I then used it to smoothly play with her anus, rubbing it in a steady circular counterclockwise motion. As soon as she began moaning and groaning, I replaced my thumb with my tongue and licked her entire asshole as though it were a lollipop.

After I had licked her asshole for at least ten to fifteen minutes, a sweet aroma arose from her vagina, and filled the room. I slowly penetrated her soaking wet vagina with my middle finger. Her vagina was now demanding attention, and some affectionate persuasion.

I rolled her over on her back, and with small bites, I kissed on her creamy yellow thighs. My arms were long enough to resume playing with her nipples, while eat her pussy all at once. I went for it, but not until she was practically screaming, "Please stop teasing me!"

I kissed the lips of her vagina ever so lightly, and I parted them with the tip of my tongue. Her juices were already flowing, and the taste of her love nectar was as intoxicating as it was refreshing. I continued kissing and licking until the hood began to recede, exposing her swollen engorged clit.

I made some space for my wide shoulders by spreading her leg a little wider and positioned myself between them. I sucked, kissed and licked her pussy to a rhythm her body could easily find, and we stuck to it. Using the suction from my mouth I got a grip on her clit and held it in the position of my liking. I continued kissing, licking and sucking in a steady rhythmical motion, until her clit exploded into a convolution of throbbing squirts. I could feel her clit dancing on my tongue as she screamed my name out loud with what was surely an expression of ultimate delight. It was clearly the highlight of her day and yet it was only the beginning of our love making.

There was a time I wasn't sure if I had a large penis or not. I didn't even care. No one had ever complained about its' size. One day I heard the joke about the guy whose penis was so long it hung in the water every time he tried to take a dump. I didn't understand the joke because I thought everybody's penis hung in the water. Mine did.

I was fully erect and ready for some good loving. I pierced her body with my tool and dug as deeply as I could get. After a couple of fumbled attempts, we were able to discover the perfect rhythm for us and she matched me stroke for blessed stroke. The clapping sound of wet flesh crashing and the moaning and groaning sounds of love making filled the room. There's a mighty thin line between making love and fucking. Tonight, that line was thoroughly blurred. I squirted semen deep inside of her as she collapsed in a heap underneath me. Not too long afterwards she fell unconscious. I also slipped into a deep restful satisfying state of slumber. Revenge could not have been sweeter. What an amazing climatic ending to a wonderful evening.

The next morning, I dreamed I was urinating while lying in the bed and awakened in a state of panic. I thought I was urinating, but Francine had my penis in her mouth and was stroking it as she sucked on it. It was the warmth and wetness of her mouth which had convinced me I was urinating. My state of panic quickly subsided and gave way to the anticipation of the many pleasures I was about to discover. I was venturing through unchartered sexual territory. I had never been awakened in such dramatic fashion. My erection was so strong a midget could have done pull ups on it. There was no question or doubt about it. I was ready to do it again.

I was about to explode once again into a trance like state of ecstasy, when she stopped abruptly and laid on her back with her legs spread wide. She whimpered, "Fuck me as hard as you can Daddy!" I mounted her with the intentions of granting her demand and pounded her pussy like my hard penis were a jack hammer breaking up concrete. There was no doubt about what this was. I wasn't making love. I was fucking the shit out of her, so she arched her back while raising her body off the bed. She found it easier to match me stroke for stroke in that position. She was fucking me back when my hot semen squirted deep inside her vagina.

She screamed my name out loud and confessed to loving me. She clutched onto my shoulders and shook a couple of times. Our mouths sought out each other as an overwhelming desire to kiss took charge. She slid her sweet tasting tongue into my mouth. I told her I loved her too. I didn't really love her. It just felt like the appropriate thing to say. I found her hospitality immensely enjoyable, so anything that would make the morning enjoyable for her, was alright with me.

After we were both spent, I rolled us a morning joint and struck fire to it. She went to the bathroom to get a couple of moist towels to wipe away our sexual fluids. As she sat beside me on the bed, I took my customary long deep draw from the joint I'd rolled and offered it to her. She shook her head and waved me off. "It's too early for me!" she said, as she held my penis in her hands, cleaning me off.

After polishing off the joint, I excused myself and went to the bathroom to finish washing up. She provided me with a new toothbrush, so I washed my mouth out with some Listerine and brushed my teeth. After getting dressed I made the necessary promises to return soon and left.

I hailed a cab and was very pleased to find Joe already up and ready for the day when I arrived at my brother's house. We walked from there, around the corner to my mother's house. As we walked, I gave Joe a blow by blow detailed description of my night with Francine. Joe was amazed by my recount of the night's events. He fell silent and was very attentive as we walked.

Oral sex was still considered taboo in the black community. Being raised by drug dealers and pimps gave me a different perspective. They all had a common saying, "Show me a man who don't eat pussy and I'll show you a man whose bitch I can snatch." In my gusto to learn the a rt of cunnilingus, I developed a desired for the smell as well as the texture and the taste of a vagina. I was hooked and Joe marveled over my openness and willingness to openly admit I enjoyed eating her ass. You could see it in his face and sense his astonishment.

When we arrived at my mother's house, she was already in the kitchen whipping up a breakfast that consisted of cheesy scrambled eggs, Canadian bacon, grits and homemade biscuits. She was quite fond of Joe and truly considered herself his aunt. She was showing love for him through one of her favorite forms of expression. Her cooking. My mother did that a lot for out of town guest.

The juice man had just made a delivery, therefore we had fresh orange juice to wash everything down. Suddenly I heard someone come in the front door. As always, I looked to my mother's eyes to confirm what I thought I'd heard. She knew I was wondering who had just let themselves into the house without knocking, and smiled before she said, "Marty... Who else?"

Marty burst into the kitchen and lit it up with her smile. Her smiling eyes found mine and gave me a personal greeting. "I got something for you baby.", she purred as she passed an envelope to me. She was excited because she had succeeded in getting a new very popular strand of marijuana for me. She had gone through a lot of trouble to get some Acapulco Gold. She knew I had never had the opportunity to smoke any before. I was more than excited to learn Marty had just given me an entire ounce of Acapulco Gold and it was all mine!

"Hi everybody!" she finally said as she turned her attention away from me.

"Don't you smoke them weeds in here. Just the smell of it gives me headaches. And you know that!" my mother protested. I promised her I wouldn't smoke the weed until I went across the street to Marty's mother's house.

I told Marty I had to change clothes, so she followed me up the stairs. I could hear my sisters helping Joe to gather the things he would need to get himself together for the day, as we climb the steps. I had to fill Marty in on everything that was going on. I wasn't afraid I was about to die or anything like that. I just wanted her to know what the whole truth was just in case anything was to happen to me. Joe followed Marty and I to her mother's house. Tab was sitting on the couch playing with her new puppy when we walked through the front door. Once she realized it was me walking through the door she squealed my name, before jumping to her feet and running to me. She wanted me to pick her up and give her a bear hug. I was more than happy to do so because I also wanted to hug her.

Joe found a seat at the kitchen table and began rolling the weed I had given him to roll. There was no one there except the family for a change on this day. I elected to hang out with Tab and play with her and her puppy she named Sparkle on the sofa. I loved Tab as though she were truly my biological daughter. Of course, in my heart she truly was my daughter.

Sparkle was a beautiful female pit bull. She was a brindle with a white diamond on her chest. I felt all the joys a young father would discover by sharing my heart and myself with this wonderful child of mine. Somehow, I understood why Tab had to come first in my life. I placed no one above my beloved child, and that included her mother or myself. I couldn't have loved her any more deeply.

We spent the entire morning, and a good portion of the afternoon, enjoying each other's company. The weed was everything I'd heard it was. To say I was pleased would be quite accurate. I was enjoying the moment but beneath the surface there was this gnawing feeling I get whenever the streets call out to me.

There still were issues that needed resolving. I had robbed my former partner at gun point, and some act of retaliation was sure to take place. I didn't know when or where but I was certain I wanted everything to play itself out in the streets. It was very important to me to avoid having any of my family members witnessing me putting in work. Observing me taking a life or being murdered would have been too traumatic for any of them. It was my way of protecting them on so many levels.

When the streets call me, I listen to her. Marty also sensed my departure approaching. I needed to shake things up. I couldn't just sit back and wait to react. That wasn't my style. Most of the time when you wait to respond to an act of violence made against you, you're already a victim. Marty had already taken a couple of pills. It was her way of dealing with the fact I took unnecessary risks in the streets. I dared the streets to take me out, but it never happened. My life at the time was fun to me only because I was under the influence of drugs most of the time and I had a twisted perception of life and the world. I had a huge chip on my shoulder and relished every opportunity to fight. I wanted to be a beast among beast and that I was. My edge was the fact I wasn't afraid to die or go to prison.

We all have this inner voice called the Self Accusing Spirit. It sounds off all kinds of alarms whenever we're about to do something against what would be considered better judgment. Most of the time my inner voice and I are in constant conflict with one another. I knew right from wrong, but I always ignored my Self Accusing Spirit and did whatever I wanted to do, and that was a great concern of Marty's. She knew there was no hesitation in my impulsive acts because I feared nothing. Whereas, others feared losing their freedom by going to prison or even dying, I did not. The fear of those things was cause for them to have a slight hesitation in their decision making. None of those things mattered to me. Come what may, was my attitude. I'll deal with whatever, whenever, however.

I had to show the world I had no fear. I felt the best way to do that would be to return to the scene of the crime and face my foes. My mere presence would be like a slap in the face and would force their hand. It would be a bold move and would call them out on the killing floor on my time, instead of allowing them to plot and plan on settling our dispute in a shootout.

As I prepared to leave, Marty begged me to be careful. I would always promise to be careful, but for the most part I ignored her pleas. It was my reckless abandonment of common sense, which I used as both an offense and defense mechanism. No one could predict what I would do from one moment to the next because I never knew. Joe and I left and began our short distance walk to the Channel one bar. I wasn't finished with my plans of revenge on June Bug and JB quite yet.

Chapter Six

The Dramatics were singing, "A Toast to the Fool" on the juke box as I was kicking ass on the pool table. While I was playing, June Bug walked in the door just as I had anticipated he would. June Bug was always a hard one to read. He always had a smirk on his face, regardless of his mood or what he was thinking. I had no idea what to expect from the conversation we were about to have, but I knew it wasn't going to end well and it wasn't going to end there. We still loved each other like brothers, but in life bad deeds are sometimes committed and they blur the vision of everyone involved. It wasn't a question of rather we loved each other or not. The question was, did we have what it took to do what had to be done despite the brotherly love. This conversation was truly a declaration of war between brothers. Respectfully.

He made eye contact with me and flashed his broad smile. He approached me immediately and took my hand in his. He shook it vigorously while all the time he was hugging me. "Let me holler at you lil bro.", he said. He placed his arm around my shoulder and lead me to the side. "I know you didn't know it at the time, but half of the money you took from JB last night was mine."

I laughed in his face and answered sarcastically, "No shit!?" For a moment, his face lost its' smirk and became flushed with anger. When the smirk returned, he spun on his heels and stomped towards the exit without uttering a word. I rushed over to the picture window and closely watch his body langue. He was angry and there was no doubt about it. It showed in his mannerism. He peeled rubber as he pulled his Thunderbird from the curb and sped down the street.

I knew his anger would drive him to go against his better judgment. I also knew he would return shortly with the intentions of initiating a shootout. He was hotheaded and hostile like that. No one knew this better than me. We had been partners since we were kids. I wanted him to find me, but not inside the bar. I wanted it to be out in the open in front of plenty of witnesses. I wanted everyone to witness the fact I was unarmed, and I had to get a gun from the guy I was walking with. I would appear to be an unarmed man defending himself, and if it were not for my quick thinking, I would have surely been assassinated.

For this to happen, I had to leave the bar at that very moment. He had a girlfriend living across the street from the bar, but he didn't go there like I had anticipated. He jumped in his car and sped away, so there was no way for me to predict his next move. To be assured the ending of our altercation would be played out on the streets, I couldn't take the chance of waiting one moment longer. Joe and I left immediately and walked slowly down Buchanan.

I was in a zone as I pranced down the street. All the while I was paying very close attention to any and everything that might alert me of his approaching arrival. My stomach was full of butterflies and my chest was tight. I had given Joe a major assignment. He was to play the role of the guy walking with me, whom I was able to get a gun from. It was that simple. All he had to do was hand me my pistol and witness how a real gangster settles his affairs about a dispute with another gangster. We had the choice in the matter. We could have settled our dispute like gentleman or like gangsters. We both chose the latter.

Marty's pleads for me to be careful hadn't fallen on deaf ears, nor were they completely ignored. I didn't feel at all as though I was taking a chance. I was more than confident I could drop them both before either of them had a chance to attempt to get off a shot. I'd practiced shooting every chance I could, and I was certain my aim would be sharp and deadly.

I spotted June Bug's car coming up the street and immediately began to time our steps according to the speed of his car. We had to pick up our pace. I wanted the car to arrive at the intersection of 128th and Buchannan just a split second before we did, and not one moment sooner.

In my mind I pictured the car cutting us off, and parking at the curb with its' rear facing us. That way, he would have to use his left hand to open the car door and his weapon would have to be in his right hand. His head, left arm and leg would be exposed once he attempted to exit the car. He wouldn't be worried about me having a weapon on me, because he had already patted me down. He was searching me for a weapon when he shook my hand while hugging me at the bar just moments earlier.

I recognized his passenger as being JB. He would have to stand up from a seated position on the other side of the car, in order to exit. Therefore, the top of his head would be exposed for less than a fraction of a second. He was already nervous because they were going up against me, and he wasn't sure it was a bright idea. He's going to duck behind the car, at the first sound of gun fire. My shot would have to be fast and sure. If the first shot missed, getting a second shot to find its mark after he ducks behind the car, would be extremely difficult. He will be a little apprehensive going up against me, but he wasn't a punk by any means. One of the things I admired most about this man was his ability to face his fears. Courage is not the absence of fear. The way he consistently responded in the face of fear, he had proven beyond any doubt whatsoever on many different occasions, that his fear was not a disadvantage.

As June Bug was parking I told Joe to hand me the pistol. I never took my eyes off the driver's door, as I held my left hand out to receive the pistol from Joe..., but Joe froze. It was long at all before June Bug and JB had successfully gotten out of the car with their weapons drawn, and the safeties off.

June Bug walked right over to us and removed the gun from the waist band of Joe's pants and ordered us to remove our jackets. I knew better than not to comply with his direct orders. I knew he would shoot anyone who challenged his authority during a robbery. As cool as we were, I'm certain it would have been Joe he would have shot.

I took off my jacket and laid it across the trunk of the car, before taking a step backwards. Joe mimicked my every move. June Bug was trying to pick up both jackets, while holding the two pistols. He was merely holding one of the pistols and had the difficult task of keeping the other pistol aimed at me. J.B. watched the entire time without offering June Bug assistance what's so ever. They had the drop on me, but he didn't trust it. He remained focused. He kept his pistol pointed at me, watched my every move like a hawk, and never said a mumbling word.

Recognizing his task as being a difficult one, I began to look for an opportunity to walk up on June Bug. I needed to make a play for the pistol he had his trigger finger on. "Back up Tone!" he ordered. He realized it was going to be difficult to hold on to the guns and the jackets, while getting into the car all at once.

We both knew the potential consequences of this confrontation could very well end with a fatality. We both feared nothing and we both were deadlier than anything in a drug store. Just as I was trying figure out a way to get closer to him, he managed to throw my pistol and our jackets into the backseat, all while keeping a keen eye pinned on me. I knew at that point he was going to get away and there was nothing I could do to stop him. I watched as he and JB re-entered his car and sped down 128th street.

I've been angry before, but it's extremely difficult to recollect ever being any angrier at any time in my life, than I was at that very moment. As I spun on my heels to face Joe, I yell at the top of my lungs, "Why the fuck didn't you give me my shit?"

"It was two against one and I didn't want you to get shot." was his response. When I looked into his eyes, I saw he had been traumatized and was in a state of terrified of shock. I couldn't believe he didn't have more confidence in me. I knew he had frozen because he wasn't ready. He had never been more afraid in his life but instead of admitting the truth, he offered up a lame ass excuse.

I was furious as we walked in silence back to my brother's house, but my anger soon subsided. I came to the realization it was all my fault. Slim saw what I'd missed. He warned me not to take Joe on any Jobs without testing him first. He saw something just by looking into his eyes that I hadn't seen even though I spent a considerable amount time with him. That was one of the main reasons I trusted Slim. His experience in the streets was immeasurable and therefore priceless.

Not much longer after we'd arrived, Slim showed up with one of his henchmen. He'd heard through the grapevine about the incident, and he was obviously furious. He took me into the bathroom where no one could hear us and demanded I give him a detailed re-account of everything. Once I'd finished Slim growled, "I'm gonna kill that Bitch ass nigga right now."

I thought he was talking about June Bug, so I pointed out the fact June Bug had the drop on me and never shot me. "I'm talking about that bitch ass nigga who froze! You're lucky you didn't get killed!" The realization was slowly absorbed but I eventually came to realize he was talking about Joe. "That bitch gonna die tonight." He turned to leave the bathroom abruptly, but I grabbed his arm to stop him from leaving.

"No Slim, it was all my fault." I went on to explain what I meant. "Don't you see it was my fault? I tried to make him into something he is not, was not, and will never be. That's what I wanted him to be and not who he is. I used to tell him stories about being in the game, and I must confess I may have glamorized everything a bit. That's because this shit is exciting to me. I can't describe the thrill I get from hustling! But, it all boils down to the fact I put him in that situation. I was moving according to the situations within each moment, on the fly. None of this was planned. He never asked to be part of this shit."

Slim grabbed me by my shoulders and made eye contact with me before saying, "I'mma tell you something right now and I'm more serious than a fucking heart attack. Before I'd allow that hoe ass muthafucka or his bitch ass ways get you killed out here on these streets, you better believe I'll kill that muthafucka myself. You should hurry up and send that little nigga back to wherever the fuck he came from. I'm through talking." He glared at me for a moment, before announcing, "I'm outta here." We left the bathroom and joined the others. He seemed satisfied after I called the bus station to see what time the next bus was leaving, so he and his giant henchman left.

My thoughts immediately returned to June Bug and JB. If they wanted to shoot me, I would've been shot. After giving the subject some considerable thought, I concluded they both would more than likely be at June Bug's woman's house across the street from the bar. I decided to go over there unarmed and get my shit. It wasn't like I was being as brave as it would appear to have been. There were always youngsters hanging around in his crib, with pistols tucked in the waist of their pants. I'd just have to size them up and decide which one was the weakest link. I was more than confident I only had to remain as close as I possibly could and claim his weapon as my own. Should the need arise, I'd simply overpower him and take it.

I told Joe I was leaving to go get our jackets, and my pistol back. My cousin Obie had just arrived and overheard what I was planning to do. He vehemently objected. "Tone you done lost it! Are you tripping or what?" He got in my face so close we were nearly nose to nose before he continued, "That's the same as committing suicide nigga! You've been acting like you're in a hurry to die lately. What's up with that shit Cuz?"

I didn't even bother to answer. What was the point? I

didn't like explaining myself to anyone, especially when it's time to put in work. I always reacted on my guts and instincts. My actions may have seemed impulsive, but my mind was made up. I was going alone.

Joe offered to go with me, but I demanded he remained behind until I returned. Albert insisted upon going with me, but I wouldn't even allow him to give me a ride. My brother had the guts, the skills, the will and the desire to assist me in whatever it was I wanted to do. Since I was going to a possible gunfight without a gun, there was no way for me to accurately predict the outcome. My answer was a resounding "No!" If I was truly marching to my death, there was no way I was going to take my brother with me. I left his house on foot and alone.

Fat Cat was a huge man. He stood about six feet four and weighed well over three hundred, and fifty pounds. June Bug's woman was his younger sister. His size and self-confidence had allowed him to become too comfortable. Once that had happened he became careless, and I caught him slipping. Fat Cat opened the door without looking or asking who it was. I could sense from his facial expression he'd been caught completely off guard, and I was the very last person in the world he expected or wanted to see when he opened the door. He quickly gathered himself as well as his composure and blocked the entrance before I was able to enter, all while he was calling out to June Bug. "Hey June Bug, Tone's here!"

"I told ya'll that crazy ass nigga was coming! Let him in.", he answered. When I entered the house, I found it full of youngsters toting pistols just as I expected. They also knew exactly who I was and displayed respect as well as affection towards me as I passed them. What they nor anyone else knew for sure was if my showing up the way I did an act of bravery, foolishness or stupidity. Time would tell.

Fat Cat lead me to the living room where I found JB and June Bug lounging. June Bug sat on the couch, while JB was relaxing in a recliner. I quickly sized everyone up in the room and chose my weapon. The loud pretty boy was my best choice, so I stood next to him.

"You one crazy muthafucka!", June Bug began. "That was some crazy shit you pulled last night. It was smooth as hell but that was some fucked up shit." I laughed and pointed out how fucked the shit he and JB did to me. I didn't appreciate getting cut out of the business and watching the money being made right in my face.

He agreed he had allowed greed to cloud his better judgment. "You're a real muthafucka Tone. There's no amount of money more valuable than our friendship. I'm sorry I pulled that shit on you. Keep the money and call it even." That was cool with me, however I decided to try to get an ongoing cut from the several houses they had operating during that time, so I inquired about how it was going to be handled.

"You done learned too much from fucking with me. That even sounds like some shit I would try. You just got cashed out nigga! You got sixteen thousand dollars and that clears our slate. That's your money back with plenty of interest."

"What about my pistol and the jackets?" I asked. June Bug told me I could have my pistol and my jacket, but that's it. They were going to keep Joe's jacket. He ordered for my pistol and jacket to be brought out to the living room. Once the youngster arrived with my belongings, he immediately handed me my jacket, and laid my pistol on the coffee table. When I retrieved it, I noticed how light it felt. "Where are my bullets?" I asked. June Bug gave me a box of shells, then he and JB gave me a hug before I left. As I was leaving June Bug got in one last undeniable dig, "Your boy's a bitch." Although I didn't agree, I left without attempting to get a word in.

As I walked back to my brother's house, I thought about what I had just done. In more ways than one, I was happy I never was given the opportunity to shoot either of them. I loved them both. It was obvious they loved me too. They never harmed a hair on my head, and they spared Joe. I loved Joe also, but I realized I'd better get his ass off the streets of Newport, before he got himself killed. I lived with a passion that most mistook as anger, but truthfully it was the level of passion I resided in. I was even beginning to impress myself, almost daily with each and every stunt I pulled.

Chapter Seven

Later that day, after I made sure Joe was on his way back to Tri City, I went to visit Unck and Auntie. They were extremely happy to see me. To my surprise Uncle Lucky was also there with his new partner, Easy. Easy was a young sharp dressing brother out of New York. We hit it off right away. He was a lot older than me, but much younger than both Unck and Uncle Lucky. Unck was the one who had convinced Easy to move from New York to Newport. Once he arrived, Unck introduced him to Uncle Lucky and the two of them became inseparable. They even became business partners.

Easy walked fast and displayed a sense of urgency in everything he did, so naturally he was sarcastically nicknamed Easy. He had brought some cocaine from New York with him, and they were blowing it. Everyone except Auntie that is. I left them and went upstairs where the kids were hanging out.

Spencer was the eldest child at the tender age of eighteen, followed by Pam who was fourteen, Herman who was twelve and Ben was the youngest at ten. Ben struggled with cerebral palsy, yet he was one of the most delightful and joyful children I'd ever met. The family own two dogs, and they were also hanging out with the children. One of the dogs was named Bruno. Bruno was a pit bull mixed with everything. The other's name was Curt and he was the largest German

Shepard I'd ever seen in my entire life! Unck told me he had Great Dane in his bloodline, and because of that he was huge and possessed the ability to lock his jaws.

Herman took to me immediately. It was as though we already knew, loved, and trusted one another. He showed me the secret to getting the German Shepard to loving you. All you had to do was give him a slice of bread with some real butter spread on it and you have a friend for life. That really was all it took to win his confidence.

Unck told me he took Curt from some people who were abusing him. He was so shaken from the abuse, if you stomped your foot in front of him, he would urinate on the floor. Everyone thought it was funny, except me. I felt his fear, and our hearts bonded.

Auntie insisted I moved in after we had a long conversation later that same day. I was able to convince Easy to give me a ride to my mother's house to collect most of my things, including my money. I explained things as best I could to my mother and gave her most of the money before moving out. Easy brought me back to Unck's house and dropped me off. He and Uncle Lucky left to go manage the now famous Hole in the Wall.

There were twin beds in Herman's room. He was more than thrilled to share his room with me. The next morning when I woke up, I felt like my bladder was about to explode, I had to urinate so badly. I had no idea Curt had laid down beside my bed and in my hastiness, I stepped squarely on his tail with all my weight. He yelped as he jumped to his feet. It startled me and for a moment I felt cause for apprehension. Curt realized he had frightened me almost immediately because of the extra sense dogs have which can detect fear.

His ability to cause me to be alarmed woke something up in him, and he became a different dog.

I had never trained a dog before, but training Curt was like second nature to me. He responded positively to everything I tried to teach him. The very first thing I taught him was to attack anyone who stamped their foot at him. I can't begin to describe how amazed everyone was with his transformation. Curt had become a totally different dog seemingly overnight. He became so devoted to me, it appeared as though I were the sole reason for his amazing transformation.

I came to love Curt like he were a person. I also sensed he had never loved anyone anywhere near as much as he loved me. All I had to do was make a gesture or issue a command, and he would instinctively know what I wanted and responded. He proved to be the best dog I'd ever had.

Everywhere I walked, I walked with my new dog. At first, I used a leash, but he became so controllable I didn't need one. I often walked him to the store without a leash and once we would arrive, all I had to do was wave my hand towards the ground and he would lay down. If I held my hand up like I was issuing a command for him to stop, he would wait patiently for my return without moving so much as an inch.

One morning just before dawn, Unck woke me up and asked if I were ready to work. He knew a fella whose girlfriend had a baby's daddy who was a bully. He was such a bully he kicked her door in, while this fella was there visiting her. The baby's father threatened to whip his ass, then proceeded to beat up his baby's momma, while the guy sat there watching. He was now willing to pay ten thousand dollars for an assassination to save face with his girl. Unck wanted to know if I would be interested in the job. I told him I was very interested, but he'd have to pay half the money up front, and the rest upon completion of the job.

Unck got in touch with the guy and made the necessary arrangements to set up a meeting. We all met up at a Big Boy's resturant and hashed out the minor details. My man was so seriously impressed by me, he was willing to pay for the entire job right there on the spot. He even offered to serve as my wheelman free of charge. An offer I graciously accepted.

He had the money on him in an envelope, and he gladly slid it across the table to me. We left there and went straight to his girl's house. I was surprised to see she was my age, but I wasn't surprised at all by her beauty. He owned one of the largest nightclubs in Newport, so she also had to fulfill the role of a trophy, suitable to present as his woman and to parade in public on his arm.

She openly stared at me the entire time we were near each other. I couldn't tell if she was attracted to me out of curiosity or if it were physical. Under any other circumstances, I would have taken this lame's woman, but this was business. I also realized she would know too much for my comfort about what I'd done to her baby's father.

After using her as bate over the phone, I cleared the modest apartment and awaited his arrival. It wasn't long before he was banging on the front door, demanding to be let in. I waited until he kicked the door in, then I escorted him inside at gun point. "I don't have any money man! I swear! You can search me." he pleaded. I assured him money wasn't an issue by escorting him to the afterlife. After wiping everything clean, I made my exit.

I found Unck and the frighten couple waiting exactly where I had instructed them to wait. Upon hearing the news about the deed being done, she began staring at me as though I had just killed the Boogie man. I don't know how many years she had been abused and terrorized by this man. I have absolutely no idea how many want to be suitors had been run off by intimidating threats of violence from him. I don't know how many want to be heroes he had beaten up. All I know is, she looked at me as though I had done the impossible.

We got dropped off once again at Big Boy's resturant. I had to force Unck to take a thousand dollars. He insisted he didn't hook me up to make any money. The guy was actually a friend of his and he was doing him a huge favor by eliminating his problem. We ordered our meal and made a salad from the salad bar. Afterwards our meals were served, and we enjoyed a hearty succulent meal.

Each booth was supplied with a miniature juke book and had the complete selection of the latest R&B recordings. I placed a quarter in the slot and turned the knob. I was then allowed to make five selections. I selected the Temptation's version of "Memories" for starters.

When we got home, I noticed my new little sister had developed a strong, interest in me. I knew sometimes young girls have no idea what it is they're feeling. Their emotions go haywire. Pam began acting like she didn't like me, but I knew what she didn't know. She used the only method she knew to get my attention. She was far too young for me to get romantically involved with, so I allowed her to do whatever she felt she had to do to get my attention, without getting angry with her.

The tolerance I had for her shenanigans is what made me realize someday she would be my woman. I have no idea how I knew, but most of the times I can sense when a certain woman will be mine. Very seldom was I wrong. Eight out of ten times I was dead on.

I told Unck and Auntie someday Pam was going to be my woman. Unk protested, "That's your sister!" I told him, "She is my sister for now, but when she gets old enough, and reaches out to me, I'm not going to turn her down!" Auntie added, "I can see it too. When she gets older, she's not going to hide her feelings for Tone. She has already confessed her true feelings to me"

I gave Auntie enough money to get Pam and Herman some school clothes. Spencer had dropped out. I then hopped on the next Greyhound bus headed to Tri City. I wanted to check on Joe, as well as lay low, until I was sure the police weren't looking for me for questioning.

Joe picked me up from the bus station. He was still very apologetic. I tried to explain to him, there were no hard feelings. "It was all my fault." I insisted. I didn't want him to feel bad, and that was one of the main reasons I wanted to spend some time with him. I felt awful after I'd realized I had put him in a situation that caused him to be frozen with fear. I got checked into a hotel and dropped my luggage off. Then we took off on our quest to check out the city, and see what the evening had to offer, as well as what we could get into.

We stopped by the neighborhood's Beer and Wine store to get some snacks, and some wine. Joe already had some joints rolled up. While I was trying to decide which wine, I noticed a woman checking me with my peripheral vision. As we made eye contact, she began blushing, yet she held her stare. I turned to Joe and asked him who the lady was. "She was gorgeous!" I flatly stated.

"Oh, that's Wendy Montgomery, Greg's wife. She won't

give you any action." He answered. He had no idea she already had done exactly that. I winked at Joe, before I turned to face Wendy. I could sense she was already mine. All I had to do was stake my claim.

I was smiling as I walked straight up to her. We continued staring at one another until I spoke. "Hello ma'am." I began. "You are such a good-looking woman! I would love to spend some time with you to get to know?" She blushed as she lowered her gaze, however there was no bashfulness detected in the tone of her voice. She told me her name was Wendy. I let her know I noticed she was checking me out. "How do you like what you see?" I asked. She smile broadly while bobbing her up and down indicating her approval as she continued checking out my physique. "Are you interested in getting to know me, or just spending some time with me?" I asked.

"Oh, I already know all about you by reputation Tone. I just wanted to know if you would be interested in attending a little gathering I'm having at my place tonight." I assured her I would be interested, and she began fumbling through her purse. She eventually produced a pen and a notepad. She scribbled down her name, phone number, and address. She ripped the page from her notebook and handed it to me.

"What time is your party starting?" I asked. She informed me it was from eight until. Which meant it was starting at eight o'clock in the evening and ending at any time we've had enough.

By now, Joe's eyes were so wide they appeared as though they were about to pop out of his skull! He couldn't believe what he was seeing. It was obvious she was openly hitting on me and didn't care who knew it. I paid for my wine, and some chips as she stood to the side waiting for me. Afterwards I walked her to her car. I wanted to see where this was leading to, and so did she. She gave me a full body hug by pressing her body firmly against mine. Once again, she made me promise to attend her party while I was still holding her in my arms. After I promised her I would, she slowly released me from her embrace. She never took her eyes off me, as she entered her car. She winked at me before she drove off.

Joe finally spoke. "Man, you don't realize what just happened. I responded by saying, "Naw, homie. You the one who doesn't realize what just happened." I tried to show him the paper with the address on it, so he could tell me if he knew the location.

Without even glancing at the paper he answered, "I know where she lives." He said it was right around the corner from his house. "What you want to do now?" he asked. "I have to give my mom's her car back. She had something to do, but she let me use it to pick you up and help you to get settled in." I wanted to see Joe's parents anyway. They were like family to me. I even called them Auntie and Uncle. Since I hadn't seen them in quite some time, I decided there was no time better than the present.

Upon seeing me, they both lit up the moment with their smiles, and gave me one of the warmest greetings I'd ever received. Just like almost everyone who knew of my athletic skills, they wanted to know if I had plans to return to school. Uncle Joe was truly one of my biggest fans. He never missed a game.

"You're too good to give up!" Uncle Joe insisted. He even mentioned the names of a few guys I used to embarrass on the basketball court, who were now playing professionally. I promised him I would seriously consider going back to school. Joe asked if we may be excused so we could go smoke and we headed to the basement.

We hung out in the basement smoking weed and listening to a new jazz group named Weather Report. They had a whole new style, and I really enjoyed their sound. The combination of the weed, wine and the music put me in such a mellow state of tranquility I soon found myself regaining consciousness. So much time had passed, it was time for the party to begin. Since the location was right around the corner, we simply walked.

When we arrived we found only a few people in attendance? You could tell they were all close friends by the way they were helping her set things up. They also were all women! We offered to assist them in any way they needed us, but they insisted things were under control, as well as insisting we sat down and relaxed at the kitchen table.

Not long after we were seated, the ladies finished the decorations and joined us in the kitchen. Wendy sat beside me and asked if I smoked weed. Before I could answer, she pulled out a joint from what seemed like thin air and lit it. She laughed as she handed it to me and reminded me that she knew me by reputation.

She left my side only to pour us a couple glasses of wine. By the time we had finished smoking and sipping the wine, the house was crowded with people. We could not have flirted with one another anymore than we had, but I was still surprised when Windy suggested we go upstairs to get away from the crowd.

"Would you like to see my bedroom?" she asked. "I have a king size bed, made for love making. I also have mirrors arranged throughout the room, so we can watch ourselves making love. Without another word being uttered, she took my hand in her own, and we got up from the table to leave the party behind!

I was admiring the décor of the red satin linen, perfectly arranged pillows and mirrors before I noticed Wendy was getting undressed. I was caught totally off guard. I noticed she had stretch marks on her stomach. I'd never been with a woman with stretch marks. All the ladies I had been with had young tight skin all over their bodies. It wasn't a turn off at all. Her body was amazing, and her beauty was a huge turn on.

She laid on her back and watched as I got undressed. I laid down on my side facing her. We began kissing and she immediately felt for my penis. Once she found it, she began stroking it, all while she was kissing me. I ran my fingers through the hair on the back of her head, as I kissed her back. For some reason I felt like we had been together before. Everything felt so natural. The sheets felt cool to my skin, and her breathing had a sexy rhythmic sound. It made me ready pounce upon her, and just as I was thinking that she tugged at my arm. She was indicating that she wanted me to mount her. We were now communicating as lovers, by using only gestures, grunts, and moans.

After I had rolled on top of her, she guided my powerfully erect penis to the moist opening. There was practically no foreplay whatsoever! She didn't want to make love. She wanted me to plunge right in, and pound the daylights out of her vagina, so I thought.

When I slid my penis inside of her, she made a gurgling sound that came from deep inside her. She was twitching and squirming, as huge tears fell from her eyes. She threw her head back, and her eyes rolled to the back of her head as she announced she was cumming. She said it so loudly, she was heard over the loud music by everyone. I'd never known a woman to cum so quickly! I still took my time to make sure her vagina got a thorough, rigorous workout. I lasted as long as I did by changing the rhythm of my strokes.

I shallow stroked her and dug as deeply as I possibly could. I kissed her tears away from her face and stared deeply into her eyes; invading her soul. I made sure she felt every bit of the caring, tenderness, and appreciation I felt, simply by looking into my eyes.

My facial expressions must have alerted her that I was about to cum, so she beat me to it. She made the same throaty, gurgling sound that she did when she first came, and started crying again. This time she whispered as she stared into my eyes, "Oh my god! I'm cumming again!" I couldn't hold back any longer. I exploded while I was still deep up inside of her. We clutched at one another tightly until the convulsions subsided.

I began to get up and rejoin the party, but she grabbed my arm, and insisted that we remain right where we were. "What about the party?" I asked.

"You are my party!" she replied and began stroking my penis once again. She was trying to keep it erect. "Do you think we could do it again?" she asked. "I wanna do it some more!" she proclaimed, and I readily complied.

After a while her friends began knocking on the door, demanding she come out of the room, and spend some time parting with them. She answered them rudely by telling them to go away. They warned her that if she didn't come out of her bedroom, they were leaving. Her only reply was, "Bye!" and we continued to make love, repeatedly. Joe later came to the door to inform us that the party was a great party, but it was over, and everyone had left. He decided to stay there, and sleep on the couch.

The thought of stopping never even crossed our minds. Once we seen the rays of the morning Sun beginning to creep through the curtains on her windows, we realized we had been making love all night long! She was such an aggressive and demanding lover. We both drifted off to sleep, entangled within a lover's embrace. It was some of the most blissful sleep I had ever gotten.

Chapter Eight

The peace and calmness of the late morning was shattered once the sharp high note of the doorbell interrupted all sleep and demanded everyone's attention. Joe hollered up the stairs to let us know someone was at the door, just in case we had somehow slept through the ringing of doorbell.

Wendy instructed Joe to answer the door, and to tell who ever it was at the door, that we were still in bed. I heard the door open, and I heard some voices speaking. However, I was unable to quite make out the words that were being spoken. After a while it was silent, but I hadn't heard the door close.

Eventually Wendy called out to Joe, "Who was it Joe?" she asked. Joe never responded, and you could sense her frustration beginning to rise. Once again, she called out, "Joe!" There still was no answer forthcoming. She then reluctantly arose from the bed, and barely covered herself with a short, flimsy, thin robe, before stomping down the stairs.

Quite a bit of time had passed before I decided to get up and investigate things for myself. This was too weird. Once again it was total silence. I still hadn't heard the door close, nor did I hear a sound coming from anyone downstairs. It was as though I were in the home alone.

When I got to the bottom of the stairs, I looked to my

right, and about fifteen feet away from me I saw a medium size dark skinned man, standing in the living room with an automatic pistol pointed directly at me. "I'm tired of you muthafuckas fucking over my family!" he yelled at me. "Ya'll doing all this shit right in front of my children?"

At that very moment, I realized who the fella was. It was Wendy's husband, Greg! There I stood before him with nothing on except a pair of pants. I was bare footed, so running wasn't an option. I had just come from upstairs which was a pretty good indication that I had to be the one who had just slept with his wife.

I had been caught with my drawers down. I had to think quickly and act just as quickly. My life truly depended on it. "What you talking about Greg? You children ain't here!" I said with confidence, because his children truly weren't there. I also used a tone of voice that express just how unimpressed I was about the pistol he was flashing.

"Calm down Greg, and tell me what your beef is with me?" I asked as I calmly strolled into the living room and took a seat on the sofa. I invited him to take a seat, which he accepted. We proceeded to have a real man to man conversation, and I was able to convince him I wasn't abusing his family. He told me that he and Wendy were divorced, and he didn't mind her moving on because that's exactly what he had done. He was about to remarry. He just didn't like the idea of his children being in the house while the house was full of grown people drinking and getting high.

Wendy finally spoke up, and for the first time I noticed her. She was cowering in a corner. "You can go upstairs and check yourself, if it would make you feel better. The only reason I didn't want you to go upstairs was because I didn't want you to see my new man lying in bed with nothing on, while you were holding that gun in your hand. The children are not her!" We both rose to our feet as he headed for the stairs to check things out. I don't blame him. If they were my children, I'd want to check for myself too.

Shortly afterwards, he returned with his pistol put away. It was the perfect time to attack him, disarm him, and keep his pistol. He had a lot of nerves to pull his gun on me, and not use it. I wanted to put a whipping on him that he'd never forget. In the past, that's exactly what I would have done. Something in my gut told me he was just a genuinely concerned father, and the right thing to do would be to understand that. I only felt compassion for the brother. Maybe I was maturing.

Greg became very apologetic, and couldn't seem to say the words, "I'm sorry." enough. I interrupted his moment to ask about Joe. He said he had warned Joe to leave, and he left out the door without saying a word.

As Greg was leaving, Joe and his dad had arrived, and were walking up to the door. Everyone knew Uncle Joe. He was born and raised in Tri City. He was not the type of man to play games. He was fun and loving, but when it came to his family and loved ones, he was no joke. I'm seriously proud to acknowledge I was one of his loved ones. Greg apologized to both of them as he passed them on the steps.

Uncle Joe asked me if I was alright. After I assured him I was fine, he hugged me, and pleaded with me to be more careful. This was the third time he had to come see about me because some man was holding a gun on me about a woman. Even though I always had everything under control by the time he would arrive, I completely understood why he was so concerned. He patted his hip where he kept a pistol. "Don't make me have to use this." he stated. He stared at me for a moment, with a huge smile on his face. He shook his head and walked away laughing.

Wendy insisted on me moving in. She said she fancied the idea of having some live-in vitamin D. I agreed to move in, so we drove to the hotel to get my things and bring them back to my new home. It was a beautiful new, brick townhouse. She also insisted that I drive the car.

I had plenty of clothes in Newport, however things were going so well I decided to purchase what I needed on the fly. At least until I was able to make a trip there, sometime in the future, to get the rest of my things. Wendy received a monthly check, and insisted that I take charge of the household, including its' finances. She brought her children home, and we became a happy family. For the first time in my life, I had the responsibilities of a man with a family depending on me, and I loved it!

I had to make sure the bills were paid, and I was responsible for the car like I was its' owner. I drove the family wherever the family needed to go. We even went grocery shopping every week to shop for wholesome foods. Wendy was an excellent cook, and together we planned the family's weekly meals.

Wendy's favorite pastime activity was making love to me. There wasn't anything left in me to share with anyone else, and I was content with that. We made love every single day! We never waited until her menstrual cycle was completely over. If she wasn't flowing heavy or cramping, she would be on me like white on rice. We even made love several times a day, at least two or three days a week. I'd never been happier.

As the months passed by, I began to realize I was happy,

but I had given up on my dream of becoming a rich man. I never considered going back to school, nor did seeking a good paying job cross my mind. The streets began calling.

Joe was desperate to prove to me that it was a fluke, when he froze on me that day in Newport. He came to me with a plan to rob a low-level marijuana and acid dealer. He said he kept about five pounds of marijuana and a thousand hits of acid on hand. The guy was a friendly hippie, with a small frame. He worked at his spot all alone, and only had a twenty-two rifle for protection.

"We can do this Tone!" he insisted. "We can pull this off and start our own business!" Of course, it wasn't him that convinced me to do it. After giving it much consideration, I was even more certain Joe wasn't cut out for this type of life, but this was like taking candy from a baby. Even if Joe froze, it wouldn't matter, because I wouldn't need him to handle whatever type of situation this hippie might create. We planned the robbery and left the house on foot to pull it off. The spot was only a few blocks away.

The setup was just as Joe had described it. There was no one there except the hippy. The only problem was, he swore he was all out of marijuana. I beat and tortured the guy until I tired, yet he swore he didn't have anything left over. There was over a thousand hits of acid, and approximately three thousand in cash. Eventually I elected to abandon my search for the marijuana, and we left. I don't know if it was because I wanted some marijuana for myself or not, I hadn't had any in days, but my gut telling me I was leaving five pounds behind. However, my gut was also telling me time was running out. We had to dip!

We made it safely to my place, and I felt it was best to

take care of our business at hand, before celebrating. We had enough to start selling acid, but it was my belief that the money was in selling marijuana. Marijuana cost one hundred and thirty dollars a pound, so we decided to take out six hundred, and fifty dollars to purchase five pounds of marijuana, and split the reminder right down the middle. We ended up with over eleven hundred apiece.

We decided to take my car and make a road trip to the city we called "A squared" the following day, to purchase some marijuana. We've always been able to find high quality marijuana in Ann Arbor. Things were beginning to look pretty good.

While Wendy was upstairs bathing the children, I placed all the acid inside a small brown paper bag, before hiding it in the corner of the highest cabinet in the kitchen. Joe and I both took a hit of acid and left the house to try to find some marijuana. It seemed like there was a drought of some sort going on, because we had a very difficult time trying to find some. It was enough to reinforce my notion that marijuana would sell very well at that time. The supply was low, and the demand was high, and that's simple economics.

We eventually found some. It wasn't the best, but it was good enough to get the hanks off. Remembering there were no papers at home, prompt me to stop at the store. I also purchased a few household items for the house, as well as some wine knew Wendy enjoyed drinking.

Wendy had already put our children to bed by the time I made it home. I rolled a few joints since I was the best roller among us. Wendy squealed with delight as she unpacked the bags to put everything away. "Thanks baby!" she yelled from the kitchen. "I love you so much! You always think of me." I told her I loved her too. It was obvious she had found the wine she liked so much. I placed the Crusaders latest album on the stereo's turntable. I really did enjoy my life with Wendy. The only thing I had to do was handle my business to sew Tri City up. Then I would have it all.

Joe left right after he had smoked a joint with us. He didn't say anything about where he was going, but I knew he would be up all night. The acid was good, and once it kicked in, Wendy took full advantage of the fact I couldn't sleep. It turned out to be another all-night session of making love.

The next day we went to Ann Arbor just as we had planned. We spent the entire day searching for five pounds, and we weren't successful at finding so much as a single pound. One guy told me he was expecting a shipment that night, but the shipment never showed up. The last time I checked with him, he told me the package still hadn't arrived, and I should check with him in the morning. We decided it would be best for us to return at some other time, and disappointedly headed head home.

I hadn't been back in town for more than ten minutes, when Wendy's sister pulled up along beside me in her Eldorado Cadillac. She rolled down her window and shouted to me with urgency. "They had to rush Wendy to the hospital in an ambulance. Follow me to the house, and I'll give you all the details." She rolled her window up and speed off. I followed her in hot pursuit.

I pulled up in front of the house, and quickly hopped out the car. I told Joe I'd catch up with him later. He understood my situation and waved as he started walking in the direction of his home. "Call me if you need me cuz." he yelled.

I didn't even acknowledge his offer. All I could think

about was Wendy. My heart raced, as I slowly became overwhelmed with fear. I rushed into the house and walked right into an ambush. Two of Wendy's older brothers and her youngest brother were lying in wait for me. The younger of the two older brothers was named Donald. He was armed with a sawed-off shotgun, and had it pointed directly at me.

Donald was not as tall as me, but he was much heavier. He had a high yellow skin complexion, with grey eyes. He never smiled, and he had the reputation of being the town's violent nut job. He was clinically insane and had just been released from prison after serving time for manslaughter.

They all sat around me in the living room, after I was ordered to have a seat in a chair. I was then informed of what was going on. While I was out of town, Wendy went to a bar. While she was there, she had a mental breakdown. She jumped up on the bar and stripped naked. She took everyone's drink from the bar and began throwing them at the mirror on the wall behind the bar. She then began busting whole bottles of liquor against the mirror.

She had to be restrained, and was taken to the hospital in a straitjacket, where she had to undergo some tests to see if she had been drugged. Her brothers and sister believed she had been drugged, because of her erratic behavior. Donald had been silent the whole time. When he finally spoke, he said he heard I'd been selling acid that morning before I left town.

I admitted to selling acid, but I denied giving any to Wendy, and I hadn't. He told me that Wendy was going before a judge in the morning, "If the test proves that she's been drugged, I'm going to blow your muthafucken ass away, right where you sit." I had no doubt in my mind if he meant every word.

At that time Ernest interrupted, and protested about the treatment I was receiving. "Tone loves Wendy! He would never do anything to hurt her." He pleaded. He didn't want any part of anything that was going on, and he made sure everyone knew where he stood by apologizing to me. When he realized he wasn't going to be able to convince them of how wrong they were, he left. When he left, the only person who didn't want to see me dead walked out. I never believed Ernest would get me help. He wasn't a snitch, and besides, they were his siblings.

I sat in silence as I listened to them plot my murder. In the morning, Wendy's sister would go to court. After she's heard what the judge's ruling was, she would call the house from a payphone. That's when we would find out if she had been drugged or not. If the judge says the report shows she's been drugged, then Donald would shoot me in the face, and simply leave me there.

In the meantime, they were going to hold me hostage. The oldest brother pulled out a pistol, and ordered me to move to the easy chair, and added, "Get some sleep." Needless to say, I didn't sleep a wink. Donald had this faraway look in his eyes. You could tell he wasn't the sharpest pencil in the box. He had a look in his eyes that made him look like no one was home. He was trying to physic himself up to perform the dirty deed should he have to. He kept saying over and over, "I will kill you about my sister." Only a fool would close their eyes under those conditions. I don't know about anybody else, but I want to see death knocking at my door. I've been able to avoid dying several times, just because I saw it coming. I wondered all night long if Wendy found the acid I hid and took a hit before she went out. If she did, I would certainly be shot in the face with Donald's sawed-off shotgun.

Around eight thirty that morning Wendy's sister left the house headed to court. I hadn't taken my eyes off any of them all night. I kept praying, and the message "All will be well." was placed on my heart. All night long they did things trying to unnerve me, but I knew I had nothing to worry about. To me their threats were nothing more than mere empty promises created out of fear and would die unfulfilled. They were afraid for Wendy, and so was I, but before the night was over, they knew I was not afraid of them, nor was I afraid of dying.

Suddenly I was startled by the sharp ringing of the telephone. The oldest brother answered the phone. He talked for a moment and hung up the phone. "I'm sorry man. I feel horrible. Ernest was right. They said she had a mental breakdown, and there were absolutely no drugs found in her system. They're transporting her to the Sanitarium as we speak."

There was not a trace of remorse in Donald eyes. He knew he had crossed boundaries with me he didn't have to cross. He wasn't sure my willingness to forgive them was genuine, even though I accepted their apologies. Nothing could've been further from the truth. I understood, because I too have sisters.

As they were gathering their things and preparing to leave, I told them that I was leaving too. I threw all my belongings in some garbage bags. After giving the eldest brother all the keys, I struck out walking to Joe's house. It was right around the corner.

After describing to Joe and his family what I had been

through, they all understood why I elected to leave. I told them of my plans to get a hotel room and stay there until I found out what was Wendy's prognosis. They would have none of that, and insisted upon me staying, as a quest in their home, for as long as I needed.

After a few days, Joe's mom insisted that we take her car, and go somewhere. She told us to just get out the house. It seemed like she was kicking us out the house, but she knew all I had received from the Sanitarium, was a daily dose of bad news. Before we knew anything, the door was closing behind us. Joe suggested that we catch up with Alvin Raff, and hang out with him and his brothers. It was a great idea.

We caught up with him at his brother's house. To my surprise Alvin's brother had moved to an apartment directly behind the Sanitarium. As we were getting out the car I noticed the view of the back of the building. I was supposed to be doing something to get her off my mind, yet here I was about to spend the afternoon, literally a stone's throw away from her.

I was glad to see Alvin again, and it was easy to tell he and his brothers were happy to see me as well. I hung out with them for quite a while. We shared war stories and made plans for him to come visit Detroit. Whereas I tried to make Joe something he wasn't meant to be, I didn't have to do that with Alvin.

While in the mist of trading war stories, Alvin explained to me how the game of chess sharpens your mind and increases your strategy planning abilities. He taught me as much about chess as he possibly could in one afternoon. He then suggested that we pack our bag and take a trip, while we listen to music, and play.

In layman terms, it meant "Let's take a hit of acid, and play chess while we're so high we are actually tripping." We did just that.

I had a great time, but as we were leaving Wendy's sister pulled up, and blew her horn trying to get my attention. She told me that the doctor told her, for Wendy to get better, I had to stay away from around the building. Wendy saw me through a window and had an episode. She went from bad to worse.

After she pulled off, Alvin and Joe began laughing. They said I was too gangster for Wendy, and it was my lifestyle that drove her crazy. It wasn't funny to me, yet I concealed my true feelings from my peers. Since I had been raised by hustlers and pimps, I was taught it was a sign of weakness for a man to display compassion or empathy towards a woman. Likewise, I was taught to never shed a tear over a woman.

I loved Wendy, and what she was going through was not amusing entertainment for me, but for some reason I couldn't openly admit it. It wasn't that I feared I'd be ridiculed by my peers. Worst of all, I felt like crying, but because of the way I was raised, I suppressed those tears. By doing so, I hid the overwhelming emotional turmoil I was experiencing. I felt I had no other logical choice than to return to Newport. Even though I was leaving, I was leaving a huge part of myself behind. I had a five by ten portrait, and images of Wendy and moments we shared seared onto the memories in my heart. That was all I had to remember her by.

Chapter Nine

When I arrived in Newport, I went straight to my mother. I sat down with her and told her the entire story. My mother began to cry as I told the story, and I remember thinking she was crying because of the heart-breaking story. That wasn't the case at all. "You were almost killed! I don't know if I would have been able to go on if I lost an one of ya'll, and I almost lost you!" She wrapped her arms around me, placed her head on my shoulders, and continued weeping while thanking Jesus. I'd never felt more loved by my mother than I did at that very moment.

I told my mother the truth about how I felt about Wendy, and I proudly took her portrait out. The portrait captured just how beautiful of a woman she was. "Oh my! She is pretty!" was momma's immediate response upon seeing the picture. She took the picture from my grip and placed it upon the empty space on one of the end tables.

I didn't want to fight the tears any longer. I excused myself and went upstairs to be alone. All I wanted was a moment alone to relish in my feelings, instead of suppressing them. A moment not to fight tears trying to burst from within a wounded heart, and damaged soul. I was tired of fighting and going against the grain. It was Friday night, and I'm sure all the spots were jumping. I was equally as sure the never-ending party across the street at Biggum's house was going down. All I had to do was call Unck, and he would have been thrilled by the news of my return.

More than anything, I was sure I wanted to be alone. I wanted to grieve the life I'd left behind. I laid across one of the empty beds, in one of the empty rooms, and for the first time, I wept. I cried for myself. I cried for Wendy. I cried for "us". I cried because I was angry over the way Wendy's brothers had treated me. I fell asleep before I realized it. A much-needed deep sleep, I might add.

The next morning while lying on the floor watching television, I heard someone knocking at the door. My mother's front door was made mostly of glass, so you were able to see who was at the door without opening it. I was totally shocked when I realized it Wendy and her two children. I jumped up, and ran to let them in.

"How did you find me?" I asked as they entered the house. All she was able to tell me was she somehow found the address. Her hair was a mess and stood up all over her head. She had a couple of suitcases and was wearing what appeared to be an old tattered housecoat. Her appearance was not impressive to say the least. She looked a hot mess.

My mother came into the room, and I introduced them. My mother was so happy to meet her, and she really took to the children. She showed Wendy the bathroom and gathered some towels, so she could bathe. Then she began fussing over the children and fixing them some breakfast to eat.

I asked my mother what I should do. She answered, "Baby you shouldn't leave someone just because they become ill". I protested and explained how she was not the same woman I fell in love with. She had a faraway look in her eyes I didn't recognize. I believed she was crazy and about to snap at any moment. My mother insisted she was not crazy. "She just sick Boo, and once she gets some help, she'll be just fine." She concluded by saying I had to be a man and learn to accept the bad with the good.

While we were having the discussion, Wendy came out of the bathroom, and the transformation from a hot mess to a beauty queen was complete. She was back to her beautiful self again. Just as I found myself beginning to feel thankful she had come my mother began insisting that Wendy call her family. Considering all that had happened, and the fact that she had escaped from the hospital, it was easy to understand why she was reluctant to contact them. She was afraid they would insist upon her returning to the hospital, but she placed the call anyway.

We weren't sure if she would have to return to the hospital, so my mother suggested we go for a ride, while she watch the children. It was to give us some time to spend alone together. I drove her everywhere! We stopped by the Hole and had a few drinks while playing pool. Afterwards we went down the street to Aunt Elizabeth's house.

I introduced her to everyone, and Wendy asked if she could use the telephone to check on the children. I dialed my mother's number and handed her the receiver. After her brief conversation with my mother, she told me her family had arrived. My mom assured her their needs were taken care of, and they were patiently waiting. I didn't trust those people at all! Especially around my family so we left immediately. We were within walking distance, so we arrived in a matter of minutes.

I recognized her sister's car as we were pulling up. They

must have noticed us, because I overheard someone in the crowd announcing my arrival. It seemed like there was a crowd of people sitting on the front porch, watching her children play with the neighborhood children and my little sisters.

Donald greeted me, and for the first time he offered his apologies. "I see I was all wrong about you man. You're not like most young guys your age. I hope there is no animosity in your heart towards me. I was only trying to protect my family, and I was wrong." I accepted his apology, and we did a soul brother handshake to seal the deal. Everyone applauded. Things could have really gotten ugly between Donald and me if we had clashed. We made peace with one another, and everyone knew it meant a possible physical confrontation had been averted.

I looked around to see who was there, in addition to Donald and Wendy's sister. Her husband and oldest brother were there and appeared to be having a great time. Ernest was all smiles when we made eye contact. We shook hands, as we embraced one another. Words weren't necessary. Ernest was the only one who defended me, but to be fair, he was the only one who knew me.

They all tried their best to convince Wendy to return to Tri City and go back to the hospital. They wanted her to resume getting the treatment she so desperately needed to recover. She flat out refused, but they were able to convince her to allow Greg to take the children home with him. They got in the cars with the children, and left Wendy behind. I didn't mind. She was beginning to act like her old self again, and that was a welcomed surprise.

We hung out all day. That night as we rode down Jefferson

Avenue, headed for the park she asked me if she could fulfill a lifelong fantasy. I was feeling up for just about anything; especially after having such a great time with her. Quicker than you could've caught a pair of thrown dice in a crap game, she was butt asshole naked! I didn't even have an opportunity to respond.

"Whoa baby whoa!" I said. "We got weed in the car, my license ain't straight, plus I have a pistol. She laughed, and continued to enjoy her fantasy, so I turned down the Boulevard headed towards the bridge that lead to the park. We rode around Lover's Lane, until we found a place to park, then started taking full advantage of the situation like the young lovers we were.

We were near the river, and you could hear sound of it running. Other than the stars and the illuminating moon, it was pitch black. The moonlight did amazing things to Wendy's silhouette and her eyes. The moment felt amazing! I had my woman back. It was as though our relationship had received a second chance for happiness. Our relationship had received a reprieve. We went back to my mother's house to spend the night.

The next morning, I left Wendy at my mother's house, because I wanted to catch up with June Bug to see what he was up to. My money was looking funny, so I needed to do something. I hugged her, kissed her and promised I'd be back as soon as I got some loot.

When I caught up with June Bug, he and JB were still doing well with the one location. Doing a job was not a necessity. I didn't even bother to ask. It appeared they were still on the fast track to prosperity. I had to find something.

Having a car made it easier to get around and catch up with people. I was able to catch up with Slim.

He had moved off Woodward to a house on Wabash. He was also down to just one hoe living with him. I don't know what happened, but I had shown up just in time. He also needed to do something to get some money, but he had a plan. He only needed a partner.

Before the Lottery was legal, it was a street hustle called the Policy. People would place bets on a three-digit number daily. You could win five hundred dollars by placing a one dollar bet or go as low as winning fifty dollars by placing a bet for one cent. In New Port's black community, the Policy was better known as the Numbers, and there were Number houses where you could go place a bet. Slim planned to rob the number house around the corner from the mother of his hoe. He told me the layout, and the plan. I felt it was a great plan, so we decided to pull off the job the next day.

I hadn't seen my brother in a couple of days, so I stopped by his house to check on him. I was on my way to pick up Wendy, but I had to pass Albert's house to get there. I figured another twenty minutes wouldn't make a difference. We had the entire evening to share.

When I walked in the house, I saw my cousin Obie, and some of my brother's friends sitting around the dining room table smoking marijuana. There was an empty seat, so I sat down to join them. "Where's Albert?" I asked. Obie told me he was in his bedroom. When I called out his name, they all hushed me, and told me he was in there with a woman.

We continued to pass the joints around, as we had the typical conversations about sports, music, politics, and religion. Eventually my brother emerged from the room, but as he exited, his roommate got up from his seat, and went in the room. I was happy to see my brother, but it was obvious they were running a train on some girl. It wasn't a surprise, because they did it all the time. I never joined in. It just wasn't appealing to me, in so many ways. They stopped asking me if I wanted a turn a long time ago, because my answer was always no. Obie was the last one out of six to take a turn, and he stayed in the room much longer than the others.

Finally, Obie came out of the bedroom, and my entire being exploded into humiliating heart-breaking pain, once I realized the girl they were running a train on, was Wendy. Obie sat down, and Wendy sat on his lap, before announcing they were in love, and she was his girl now.

Everyone burst into laughter, except me. "How you gonna fall in love with a bitch, after we all of us done fucked her?" Albert asked. My heart sunk. I had been totally betrayed. Not only by some of my so-called friends, but my first cousin and my brother as well.

"We gonna need those car keys too cuz." Obie added to their announcement. I said okay as I handed him the keys. As they were leaving, I told them they had better make my momma's house their first stop, so they could get her things. Obie said they were planning for her to stay with my mother, until they could find somewhere to stay. I let them both know there was no way in this world I was going to allow her to stay with my mother. He didn't want to understand why his new girl couldn't stay with his aunt until they found somewhere they could stay, so I gave them some incentive. I told them if they hadn't gotten her things out my mother's house by the time I got there, I promised them I would burn everything single stich in the middle of the street. Suddenly he understood.

I went to Biggum's house, bur Marty wasn't there. For some reason Biggum was trying to get me to stay for a while. She really loved me like a mother loves her son. She just wanted to talk, and that's exactly what we did. We talked until about three in the morning, before I called it a night. I went across the street alone. That wasn't the plan, but that's the way things turned out. My girl left me for my cousin, after being gang banged. I wondered how I could show my face or hold my head with dignity, as I'd always done once the details of the. It was sure to get out that on this day my ego was shattered, and life humbled me. I was glad I didn't have to explain to my mother what had happened. She really liked Wendy a lot.

The next morning, I was on the block trying to hail a cab, to get to Slims' house. I had told him just the day before, I didn't need a ride because I had a car. Suddenly the bus arrived, so I jumped on it. I had no shame using public transportation. I had to get to Slims' crib, and I was determined to get there by any means. We had an appointment with a certain Numbers house, and it was imperative we kept it. As I was walking up Wabash I noticed Wendy's car parked in front of Slims' house. Wendy and Obie were there.

Slim answered the door, and with a chuckle said, "Obie says he snatched your woman, and now they have to stay with me because you won't let her stay with your momma." Obie had absolutely no hustling ability. His idea of hustling was asking somebody for a couple of dollars. He lived with his mother and he knew there was no way he would've been able to convince his mother to allow Wendy stay with them.

He knew better than to ask her, so he didn't waste his time. I wondered where they would stay, and now I knew.

"I ain't got time for the bullshit Slim. You know I've always been about getting money. That's the reason I'm here. What time are we going to go collect our cash?" I asked. I didn't act as though I was bothered by their presence. I spoke to both and laughed to myself. I knew it would only be a matter of time. I didn't even recognize the look she had in her eyes. She was about to lose her mind. She wasn't my problem anymore. The pain I had experienced, because of their betrayal, was enough to help me dismiss any concern I once had for her wellbeing. I truly only cared about getting the money from the robbery Slim and I had planned.

Policy was a big deal back then. Whenever you robbed a numbers house, you were robbing the Mafia. They were famous for finding out who committed the robbery and murdering the culprit. The fear they generated was enough of a deterrent for most, but not for me! I looked forward to a possible confrontation with the Mafia. I had decided long ago, I wanted to die a legend, and street legends don't fear dying.

We entered the house through the front door. Neither one of made any attempt whatsoever to hide or cover our true identities. We pretended to be the police. That is until this old man told me he knew his rights, and he didn't have to follow my instructions to get on the floor. I slapped him across his nose so hard it opened a deep gash on its' bridge. He went to the floor, with his hands cupped beneath his nose in a pointless attempt to catch the running blood.

There was some mumbling in protest over the treatment of the old man, so I decided to clear up the misunderstanding.

"Okay, ya'll done figured out by now we ain't the muthafucken police. This is a robbery. We don't want to hurt anybody, but as you can see, we will. Just cooperate, and we'll be out of here before you know it." From that point on, the job was easy.

We went back to Slims' house to count and split the take. There was well over fifteen thousand, so we were able to pocket nearly eight thousand apiece. Slim and I began making plans to celebrate. We had dared to rob the Mob and were successful at doing so. My pockets weren't big enough to hold all of my money, because most of it was in small denominations. I had to put some of it in a brown paper bag, and I carried it like it was my lunch. Slim suggested that we go to the mall and get sharp. "Let's get sharper than a muthafucka and paint this town red! I need some more hoes, and I can hear some bitches calling out my name right now!"

I had already talked to Slim about taking me to my mother's house. I wanted to drop off all my big bills and take only the small bills to the mall. My mother was sitting on the porch when we pulled up. We all got out of the cars to go into the house. I greeted my mother, and the look she had on her face said it all. She was worried about me. Obie spoke, but her only response to him was, "I'm so ashamed of you."

She took my hand, and led me into the house, as she glared over her shoulder at Obie. She told me to go to the kitchen, which was as far as you could get from the front of the house. "I heard about the whole thing. Are you alright Boo?" she asked. She proceeded to search my eyes, looking through the windows of my soul, to see if I would try to lie, so I didn't.

"No momma. I'm not alright. I'm so embarrassed and ashamed. She took me in her arms and asked me what it was I felt. I really had no idea how I felt. I was numbed by the pain

I suppressed. "How could any girl I loved, do something so horrible like this to me momma?" I asked.

"No! She didn't do it to you baby. She's sick. They took advantage of the fact that she's not in her right mind. It had nothing to do with her making a decision to do those things in her right mind. Try your best to understand. She's sick!"

"Okay, even if that is the case, what about my friends, Albert and Obie? They're not sick."

"You're right. Sometimes people do sick shit baby." We stood there in silence for a while before I spoke.

"When everybody finds out what happened, I'm gonna feel so ashamed. My girlfriend went behind my back and had sex with six different dudes, momma. One right after another. One of the dudes was my brother, and when she was through with everybody, she decided she would rather be with my cousin than me! The fact I was there the whole while it was happening, but I was too dumb and slow to see what was going on, may be the most embarrassing part about it all. How can I show my face after all this gets out?"

"I don't understand why you feel ashamed. You didn't do anything to be ashamed of. You didn't know what was going on, because those who were in on it, made sure you didn't see anything. You can't blame yourself for not being able to see through walls Boo. Not only can you show your face, but you should hold your head high. I know the truth, and the whole story, and I'm very really proud of you."

She warned me that it was already out. According to her, everybody was talking about it, but she made me promised I wouldn't allow it to make me do something that would ruin me. I went upstairs to put my money up, and momma went back out to the porch.

When I made it back to the porch, Momma was still cussing Obie out. She was trying to explain to him how wrong it was to take advantage of a sick girl. She told him he shouldn't deliberately hurt family. Obie never said a word. He just hung his head low and walked back to the car. I told momma I'd see her later and hopped in the car with Slim. Off to the mall we went, with our pockets full of cash.

Chapter Ten

I spent lavishly at the mall. Making sure it was obvious money wasn't an object for me. Since I was spending small bills, I looked like I was carrying a humongous amount of money. Every time I pulled my bank roll out to pay for something, Wendy and Obie would watch my every move. It was as if they expected something from me. If they were expecting something, they were rudely awakened and disappointed. I did not contribute so much as one red cent, to or towards them.

I guess that within its' self was proof I was salty about my cousin taking my girl from me. It didn't matter that she was sick. I didn't care! Slim brought them a couple of things, and that seemed to please them. It's a good thing he did, because I wasn't about to extend such an olive branch. We made plans to go out that night to the Royal York night club. I'd plan on buying them a drink at the club, and toasting their new-found love as I scanned the crowd in search of her replacement. -

Slim dropped me off at my new home with my new things. He wanted to come in, but he had to go get ready, and so did I. Unck wasn't home, so I hopped in the shower, and got decked out in my new threads. I checked myself out in the mirror, and I had one of those rare moments where I actually looked fabulous to myself. I had a feeling some gorgeous woman was going to try to mend this broken heart. The way I was looking tonight, all I had to do was to be seen.

That night the Royal York was jumping. I was higher than any young man should have been. I had taken a hit of acid and smoked some magnificent Acapulco gold. Upon my arrival I threw down several shots of gin, but I was so high off the acid I couldn't feel the drinks.

I was having a great time! I danced so much and hard, I was sweating. That's when I noticed a woman sitting at a table all alone. I couldn't understand why she was alone. She was so lovely I wasn't sure I processed what was necessary to interest a woman of her caliber. There was no doubt about her being a full-grown woman.

Slim, Obie, and Wendy were watching me closely, so I decided to go for it. I was going to make a play for this beautiful doll, since I had an audience. It was a great opportunity to test my game.

"Hello." I said as I walked up to her table. As noisy as the bar was, I knew there was no way she could have heard me. She had been staring at me from across the bar, and she watched me as I slowly walked up to her table. She read my lips, and lightly patted a seat next to her. As I sat down beside her, I got a really good look at her, and she was much better looking up closely.

She had a light skinned completion, with a red hue. I didn't know if it was the red lighting in the bar that enhanced her Indian features or not, but there was evidence of Native American somewhere in her bloodline. Her hair fell well below the middle of her back, and was thick, jet black and wavy. Her eyes were dark and framed by perfectly arched eyebrows and long flirting lashes. Her cleavage was exposed, and its' jiggling was all the evidence I needed as proof of them being big, real, and delightful. Her hips were wide enough to fill her seat, but her waist was tiny. She had a thick body, with long shapely legs.

We tried to hold a conversation over the loud noise of the crowd and loud music, but we were unable to do so. The more she stared at me, the more apparent it became she was enjoying the view. I suggested we step outside and get to know one another. She too wanted to get away from the noise she readily agreed. When she stood up, what I saw made my heart pound. I had never seen a buttock a pair of legs and thighs look so perfectly shaped. Slim and Obie were watching with a look of astonishment on their faces. Wendy appeared to be sincerely happy for me. My new friend seemed as pleased as I was to be leaving together

Once we were outside, she opened up to me. Her name was Netta, and she was once madly in love with her husband, but he had passed away suddenly and unexpectedly from a mysterious illness five years prior to the date. She had two beautiful children, and she devoted all of her time and energy towards raising them. She had gone out for the very first time since her husband had passed. She was looking for a man to be nothing more in her life than a lover. He had to look a certain way and have the stamina to last an entire forty-five minutes.

As fine as she was, I was more than sure I would be able to last for the entire forty-five minutes or maybe even more! All I needed was an opportunity to prove it. She asked me to walk her to her car. "There's no need for me to sit around here any longer. My search is over! I believe I've found what I'm looking for." she said as she handed me her car keys. I quickly opened her car door and smiled. "You're quite the gentleman to be so young! Who taught you your manners?" she asked. I told her pimps taught me everything I knew, and my answer caused her to burst into laughter. "A sense of humor too! That's another plus."

She handed me a piece of paper with her phone number written on it. She placed a hand on the side of my face, and our lips slowly closed the distance between them until they met. She gently parted my lips with her tongue and slid her tongue into my mouth.

Although it only took a moment, the kiss felt like it lasted much longer. She sat down in the driver's seat afterwards. "I gotta go." she said as she placed the keys in the ignition and started her car. I tried my best to convince her we had enough time to get together that night, and I could still be gone before her children could awaken. She closed her door, rolled down her windows and said, "Be patient my darling." As she pulled the car away from the curb she yelled, "Call me when you get home."

When I went back in the bar, I found Slim quite irritated. He was ready to leave, because there were no sporting ladies in attendance. Slim wanted hoes, and since there were none, he was ready to go. I was ready to go as well. I couldn't get to a phone quick enough. I knew I could convince Netta to come and get me tonight, if I could get to a phone before it got too late. Obie and Wendy didn't look like they cared one way or the other, so we all left.

As soon as we walked into Slims' door, I picked up the receiver from the telephone, and dialed the numbers Netta had written on the small piece of paper. She answered the phone on the first ring. I don't know if it was because she didn't want the ringing of the telephone to waken the children, or was she waiting and hoping I would call. This time the entire conversation was of a sexual nature. We felt each other out by asking the customary questions asked when you are about to become intimate with a new lover.

It wasn't long before we were talking raunchy. She described the type of penis she liked, and what she wanted to do to it. I kept telling her, "You know you want me to dig in that nappy dugout. You'll feel me all up in your stomach!" At one point she had stopped talking completely, all while she was making some throaty groaning and moaning sounds. My ego would like for me to believe my conversation was so hot and heavy she had to touch herself, and once she did it was too good for her to stop, nor could she speak.

When she found her voice, she asked where she could pick me up. We both agreed upon the Grand River and Buchanan location, because it was only a five-minute drive for her, and a five-minute walk for me. Her last words to me were, "I'm leaving out the door right now. You better be there Tone!"

As I was arriving, her black Pontiac Bonneville was pulling up. We both were displaying broad smiles. She was seated behind the steering wheel, but she slid across the red leather seat to the passenger's seat and said, "You're driving." After getting seated behind the steering wheel, she instructed me to head towards the Edison District. While smiling at me, she stated, "I'm serious Tone! If you don't fuck me for at least forty-five minutes, I'm never gonna fuck you again. You sure this ain't gonna be the last time?"

As we rode, she opened up some more. She hadn't been sexually intimate with anyone the entire time she'd been mourning. All she did was masturbate and play with toys. She was very explicit as she described her method of masturbating. It was like she was performing a ritual with all the details.

We finally reached our destination, and I pulled the car into her driveway. Her home was nothing extravagant, however it was a very attractive, comfortable looking and modest. She asked me to walk lightly as we entered the house. We were trying to make sure we didn't wake the children.

Her bedroom was well lit, although there were only blue lights. She began disrobing immediately. She told me the only thing she did was drink wine, but I could smoke some weed if I wanted.

There were two empty wine glasses sitting on her dresser and sitting on the floor alongside her bed a bucket of ice was chilling two bottles of wine. She opened the bottle and filled the two glasses. She began drinking, while I rolled myself a fat joint.

After I had smoked a joint, and drank a couple of glasses of wine, I stood and began removing my garments. She stopped me and pleaded with me to allow her to do it. The Isley Brother's newest release, Who's That Lady, was playing on her eight-track tape player while she undressed me. Every time she removed a garment, she would shower the exposed skin with a flurry of light kisses.

She laid on her back, as I mounted her in the missionary position without any foreplay. She insisted she was ready to get right to it and was not in need or the mood for any warming up. Her hair was spread all across the pillow, and her breast were spread all across her chest. She had the largest breast of any woman I had ever been with, and her nipples were thick, dark, and inviting.

I slowly worked my penis inside her vagina and began

sucking on those delightful nipples. I was totally memorized by the moment. She was very stiff in the beginning. When I first inserted my penis, she became as rigid as an ironing board. It was kind of like a confirmation she hadn't had a man in years. Once she had gotten loosened up, and got it going, she became a real live hot wire. She was sucking on my tongue and holding me so tightly, her finger nails dug into my skin and drew blood. She rose her buttocks up off the bed, to assist me by positioning her vagina so I could dig a little deeper.

Just when the motion was exactly as I liked, she suddenly stopped, and rolled over on her stomach. She rose up on her knees and asked me had I ever done it from behind before. I told her the truth. I hadn't. "Don't put it in the wrong hole." was all the instructions she gave me. She took my penis in her hand and rubbed its' swollen head against her swollen clit. We both were beyond ready to resume the intercourse, so she guided my shaft back inside her vagina.

I was thinking "Oh my god! This is amazing!" I'd never done it that way before, and it seemed like the shadows from the blue lights were enhancing the loveliness of her perfectly shaped ass. I really went at it, but every time I felt as though I were about to ejaculate, I would wonder had it been forty-five minutes yet, and I held back. Eventually I was unable to hold back any longer. I exploded and spilled my semen deep inside of her. I had ejaculated harder than I'd ever ejaculated in my life!

She collapsed and rolled over on her side. She took my hand and guided it towards her soaking wet vagina. She wanted me to finger fuck her, and she said so. "Damn! You have big strong hands." she purred. Using both of her hands, she got a firm grip on my wrist, and began fucking two of my fingers. She begged me to insert another finger, so I forced it in. She begged for more, so I inserted my remaining finger. With all four of my fingers now inside of her vagina, she screamed, "Oh yes! That's it! Please don't stop! Please!"

I noticed she was no longer afraid we would awaken the children. Her vagina was squeezing my hand so tightly, it took real concentration and strength for my fingers not to collapse under the pressure. All of the sudden her vagina made a strange sound. It sounded like air escaping from a balloon, as a clear liquid from her vagina sprayed my face.

I had never seen a vagina squirt before, nor did I know it was even possible for a female to ejaculate. I had never even heard of such a thing. She grabbed me and held me close and tried to hide her face. She was embarrassed and didn't want me to see her wearing the shame on her face.

"I've never done that before." she admitted. I asked her had it been forty-five minutes. She chuckled and answered, "Yes baby. We'll be getting together again. Now get dressed so I can give you a ride home, while the children are still asleep."

It turned out to be one of the most memorable nights of my life! It was only the first of many uncountable sexual encounters Nett and I would share. I'd passed the test with flying colors. She dropped me off right where she had picked me up, and I walked the rest of the way back to Slims' from there.

Obie opened the door to let me in. He quickly rejoined Wendy on the sofa, who was still sleeping. It didn't bother me in the least bit to see them together. I stretched out on the recliner and fell fast asleep. I thought about the past events. I marveled over how something so horrible could happen to me, and I was able to rebound in such a short time. I felt like I was the luckiest guy in the world, as I closed my eyes. Before I knew it, I had drifted off into a blissful slumber.

I was awakened to the sound of everybody starting their day. Slim was having a conversation with Obie. He said he felt left out, because he was the only one who had not had sex with Wendy. When Obie agreed to let Slim have sex with Wendy, Slim took her to his bedroom and closed the door. I didn't like what was going on, so I called a cab, and left to go home.

When I walked through the door, I could smell breakfast cooking. I followed the aroma to the kitchen, where I found Auntie cooking. I kissed her on the jaw and went in the bedroom to talk to Unck.

I got put up to speed about everything that had been going on since I had been gone. He had caught up with an old partner of his named Fly. "As soon as I'm dressed and eat some breakfast, I'm gonna call him and tell him to come pick us up. It's time to go to the spot and get to work making some real money son."

After telling me this he got up. I had to run upstairs, because Curt knew I was home, but couldn't get to me because the door was closed. He was going nuts! He was barking and scratching at the door trying his best to get to me. Auntie yelled from the kitchen, "Go see about your baby, son!" I answered her by letting her know I already was on my way up the stairs.

When I opened the door, Curt jumped up on my shoulders and began licking my face. I was six feet three, and Curt was taller than me when he stood on his hind legs. I hugged him petted his head and massaged his ears. He always seemed to love it, and once he'd had his fill of my loving he would hop down and sit beside me. Every step I took from that point on, wasn't done outside of his presence. He'd became so in sync with me, it was as though our steps were synchronized intentionally.

Spencer and Herman were just waking up. The aromas from the food was now drifting through the opened door. It proved to be all the necessary incentive it took for them get up. They were scrambling hurriedly to put their robes on. They ran downstairs to get something from the kitchen to eat. I jumped in the shower, and Curt laid down beside the closed bathroom door, patiently awaiting my return.

After I had gotten dressed, I stood in front of the mirror in the bedroom, smoking weed and admiring how good I looked. My thoughts were interrupted when I heard Unck asking me if I were ready to go yet. I asked him if I had enough time to walk Curt before we left. His replied, "Of course son. We'll wait." That was the first time he'd called me son. It felt good whenever Unck or Auntie called me son. I made a mental note to always address them as Mom and Dad.

When Curt and I returned from our walk, I noticed the white Oldsmobile Tornado with red interior parked in front of the house. Unck was on the porch having a conversation with an older gentleman I believed I'd seen somewhere before. He was sharply dressed in a green pastel leisure suit. He wore a Godfather hat, which matched the color of his suit. All his accessories were money green and were a great compliment for his money green alligator shoes. He wore a lot of jewelry, just like a pimp, and some gold wire framed glasses. The way he wore his shoulder length hair, made him resemble the character Priest in the movie Super Fly. Ironically his real name was Fly Wilson, but everybody who knew him or of him, call him fly. When he smiled, you were able to see he had a mouth full of beautiful pearly white teeth. The skin under his chin sagged, but that was the only indication that he was an older man. He looked, moved, and dressed just like a much younger man.

After I had put Curt away, Unck me introduced to Fly. "This is Tone, my son I've been telling you about. He reminds me so much of my father. He's just like him. This is your Uncle Fly." It seemed like he could have gone on and on about how perfect I would be for what Fly needed. We hoped in the car, and Uncle Fly placed Earth Wind and Fire's latest release, The Way of the World, in his eight-track tape player. He checked the side mirror for oncoming traffic, then he merged into traffic.

Unck and Fly were reminiscing and being brought up to speed about their respected families. We rode to a house on the corner of Pacific and Beechwood and stopped. The house was a very nice two family flat made of red brick. Fly backed the car up onto a driveway at the entrance of a garage. He got out of the car and used a key to get inside of the garage through a side door. A few moments later he reappeared. He was opening the garage door by pushing it up. Unck and I got out of the car, and I offered to help, but he waved me off. "I got it." he insisted.

He backed the car inside the garage, got out and popped opened the its' trunk. After getting a bag out of the trunk, and throwing it over his shoulder, he closed it. He closed the side door and explained that he always left the garage door open, so his car could be seen. That was a signal to his cliental that he was in. He then led us across a small fenced in backyard to a long white wooden staircase, which led to an upper flat.

We walked through the kitchen, which was poorly

equipped. You could tell from the look of things, it had been quite some time since the last meal had been prepared there. We continued to the next room, which was the dinning-room. All the walls in the room and the living room were painted black, except one wall. That particular wall was behind a black sofa sectional and was made of mirror. It made the living room appear much larger than it really was.

There were three doors in the living room. The lone door in the far corner, was the entrance. There was a full bar to the immediate left of the entrance, with a door behind it. The door behind the bar led to an attic. The other door was on a connecting wall and led to an outside porch which overlooked the front yard of the house.

Fly opened his bag, and pulled out some lime juice, and a fifth of Tanqueray. He went behind the bar and asked me if I would like a drink. He fixed me and Unck a drink and toasted to new beginning. We clicked glasses and took a sip.

Fly asked me how I liked the place. "What's not to like?" I asked. It was the perfect bachelor's crib. He gave me a tour of the place while telling me about some guy named Pretty Rick he had living there and managing the business.

I was about to ask him a question, but he cut me off before I could speak, to ask me if I smoked weed. "Hell yeah" I answered while laughing. "I can't get enough." He led me through the door behind the bar and climbed the steps to the attic. A pool table sat in the middle of the spacious attic, and was surrounded by huge black garbage bags full of marijuana. I had never seen so much marijuana before in my life. "How much weed is here?" I couldn't help myself from asking. He told me it was one thousand pounds. "Get yourself a handful, and let's go down stars so you can try it out." I realized right then, and there, Uncle Fly was rich!

As I smoked some of the best weed I'd ever smoked, he told me all about himself and his operation. He had a huge house in the suburbs, and this place was only his place of business. He sold one thousand pounds of marijuana, and one million hits of THC tablets a month.

Pretty Rick had stolen some work from him, and he wanted him to be hurt. He didn't want him killed, he just wanted him to be taught a lesson on the consequences of stealing. Pretty Rick hung out with a Professional boxer by the name of Bernard McKinley, who also was Fly's best friend. Everybody called him Big Foot. Big Foot was a top ten contender in the heavyweight division, and the personal sparring partner of the undisputed heavyweight champion of the World. Pretty Rick was a member of Big Foot's entourage.

Fly told me Big Foot was on his way with Pretty Rick. He wanted to know if I would beat him up. I had never seen the guy before, so there was no way I could guarantee a victory, and I told him as such. I told him what I could do was guarantee him was my best effort. Fly began laughing and couldn't stop. I didn't get the joke.

Big Foot showed up shortly thereafter, with Pretty Rick in tow. He seemed totally unaware of the immediate danger he had voluntarily walked into. Seeing him made me completely understand Fly's laughter. Rick was a small man. More of a petite pretty boy, than a fighter.

Fly introduced Unck and I, to Big Foot and Pretty Rick as his brother and nephew. "I know you stole my shit Ricky." Fly finally told him. Before he had a chance to deny having committed the deed, Fly issued his first order to me. "Kick his ass Tone!" I quickly snapped his head back, with a left right combination to his face. He dropped to the floor and folded up in the submissive fetal position.

I became angry because he wouldn't fight me back. The more he wouldn't defend himself, the more vicious I became. There was no doubt in my mind about this being an audition, so even though he was knocked unconscious, I continued to kick him in his face with all my might. Fly himself had to pull me off his ass. His whole face was a bloody mess. There was nothing left to admire about his looks. Fly wanted to witness my viciousness and was very pleased and impressed by my performance.

Fly asked me how old I was. I informed him I was about to turn twenty-two in a couple of days. He got excited, went behind the bar and pulled out a couple zip-lock gallon size freezer bags filled with marijuana. "Happy Birthday! Here ya go! That's two pounds. Sell one of them and get yourself an outfit on me. Then keep the money off the second pound for pocket change." At that time, it was the most marijuana anyone had ever given me. I believed it was payment for the vicious beating I had just administered. That is until he told me he wanted me to address him as Uncle Fly, as well as move in and run the place. Pretty Rick's time as the house manager had just expired.

I was more than happy for the opportunity. I was thankful. The place was only a twenty-minute walk to my mother's house. I would have a nice place of my own, in the hood. Finally! I asked Unck if Curt could stay with me, and he agreed to let me keep him.

As it turned out, Unck and Auntie had been approved for a bigger and better house and were moving. The house wasn't ready yet, so they were going to have to stay with Granny, Unck's mother, for a couple of weeks. There just was not enough room to keep Curt there. That was perfect as far as I was concerned! Curt and I were becoming more and more inseparable. We would use the time to form a bond very few would ever understand.

Uncle Fly asked me if I would mind going to the store for him to get some more lime juice, and whatever it was I wanted to drink. "You can't be drinking my Tanqueray!" he said with a chuckle. It was his way of letting me know he was joking, but extremely serious. I agreed to go to the store and headed for the door. He stopped me and asked what I was going to do for money. I had a pocket full of money, so I told him I was straight, and I'd pay for it.

"I love this boy already!" then he surprised me by saying, "I need you to get the car washed and fill up the gas tank." As he handed me his car keys. He put his hand in his front pocket and pull out a wad of money that was so big, it would've choked a mule. Every single bill was a hundred-dollar bill. He handed me one and told me to keep the change. He and Unck had a lot of business to discuss, and they wanted me out of their hair. "Take your time. Let your friends see you riding in style." I thanked him and left. I couldn't wait for my friends to see me driving the latest model of the Oldsmobile Toronado on Buchannan.

Chapter Eleven

I stopped at the car wash on Warren and Junction, and got the car washed. The usual activities were taking place. Delivery men were making deliveries, winos were begging for extra pocket change, and prostitutes were trying to flag down cars with white men in them peering through their windshields seeking instant sexual gratification for a few dollars. Buses and taxi cabs were picking folks up and dropping them off. I didn't see anyone I wanted to see me, so I stopped at the gas station on 130th and Warren to fill up the tank.

I still hadn't seen anyone I wanted to see me, so I crossed the bridge on 130th street, and headed to my mother's house. As I pulled up to the house, I noticed Marty's car parked in front of her mother's house. I wanted to see Marty for sure, but I had to check in on my mother first.

Amazingly enough, my mother was just as concerned about me. "Hey baby! You alright?" she asked, as I walked through the door. As always, she searched my eyes. I didn't waste time with words. I took her by the hand, and led her outside, so she could get a good look at the car. I had the sunroof wide open, and the rays from sun made the car look even more magnificent.

"Whose car is this?" she asked, with a serious concerned

expression on her face. I did my best to convince her the car belonged to a friend of mine. "Baby don't be out here stealing cars. I thought you grew out of that. Didn't you?" I told her the car really did belong to a friend of mine. It was funny that she actually thought I could regress to the point of joy riding.

"That's a real nice car Boo. Your friend must have a whole lot of money to trust you to drive a car this expensive!" I explained to her how my friend had full coverage, so if anything happened to the car the insurance company would take care of all the expenses. I gave her a smile a kiss and a huge hug. I told her I was going across the street to spend some time with Marty and took off headed in her direction.

Marty met me at the door, and she was thoroughly upset with me. "Why are you stealing cars? You know you can drive my car anytime you need a car!" She stood before me with a scowl on her face, and her hands on her hips. She even rebuffed my attempts to hug her, and I tried several times. I told her all about Fly, and the place I was moving to on Pacific. "That's a very nice car!" she said while beginning to show signs of calming down. "I'm looking forward to meeting this newfound uncle of yours."

I didn't want to stay away too long. I had other people I also wanted to see. I needed to spend some time with Tab. She was still the love of my life. She was getting older, but she was still my baby girl. Marty knew how much I loved her daughter. Whenever she saw Tab and I huddled up, she would leave us to enjoy one another. We had a very special bond that seemed to grow stronger with each passing day, as did our love for one another. You couldn't tell me she wasn't my daughter. She had even began calling me Daddy.

I left there and went to see Slim. Even though the chinks

I had discovered in his character had tarnished my view of him, I still loved my big brother. I rationalized everything by accepting the fact that nobody is perfect, and it was wrong for me to expect him to be perfect. I parked right behind Slims' Eldorado. I saw Wendy's car parked across the street.

They were all on the porch drinking wine, and smoking weed. I was a little disappointed to discover Obie was putting Wendy to work selling her body on the streets. Slims' fingerprints were all over this recent development. There was no way Obie's feeble mind could've come up with such a plan. Her street name was going to be Mary.

When I looked into her eyes, I could see she was losing her grip on reality. All I could do was hope nothing harmful would happen to her while she was out there working. I no longer blamed her for her actions. I finally realized she truly was ill, and why she shouldn't be held accountable for her actions or decisions. I seriously couldn't stomach any of it any more. When Slim convinced Obie that he should sample her wares, I made my excuses and dipped.

I stopped at the store on Lovett to purchase some Zig-Zag rolling papers. They were much thinner than Tops, but still burned slowly. I got excited because I seen Hope in the store. "Hey baby! How have you been" I asked. She looked at me as though I had just crawled from underneath a rock. She had an expression on her face like she smelled something awful. She rolled her eyes at me as she left the store without saying a word. I was shocked and puzzled by the way she had acted towards me. I was the only one who hadn't tried to hit on her when Fat James was arrested. I was very disappointed, because I was genuinely excited to see her again.

When I left the store, I could not believe my eyes. There

were two Hopes standing next to a car, and other than the clothing they wore, they appeared to look exactly alike! One of them was smiling, and briskly walking towards me with her arms stretched out, like she was expecting a hug. I could tell by the way she was dressed, she wasn't the woman I'd seen in the store.

She hugged me and asked me he how I'd been doing. I told her I had been fine, and then she introduced me to her identical twin sister. Her name was Faith. I laughed and explained how I thought Faith was her. Faith apologized for being so rude, and added she thought I was trying to hit on her. I graciously accepted her olive branch and returned my attention to Hope.

I asked Hope what she was up to, and she responded by informing she hadn't been anywhere, or done anything in months. I took that as a que, so I invited her to come hang out with me. I wasn't hitting on her. I just wanted to spend some time with her, and she accepted the invitation.

We walked over to the car, and I opened the door for her. She let out a low whistle, "Is this your car?" she asked. I simply told her it was my uncle's car, and she hopped in the passenger's seat. I inquired about her sister, and she stated she's cool. She has her own car. I was riding with her. I got behind the wheel, reeved up the engine and turned the eight-track player up loud to get attention, before pulling away from the curb.

My last stop was the liquor store. Hope wanted some vodka and papaya juice, and Uncle Fly wanted some lime juice. I brought everything I could think of that we might need. I even brought munchies! We were all set to have a good time catching up. I wanted to know how she and her little girl were doing. More importantly I wanted to know how Fat James was doing. I was curious about how much time Fat James had gotten. I also wanted to know in which state he was doing his time, and things of that nature.

By the time we arrived, Bigfoot and Pretty Ricky had left. Fly and Unck were the only ones there. They were reminiscing about the days when they were both mailmen. Come to find out, that's how they met.

I introduced everyone, and both Uncle Fly and Unck had something complimentary to say about Hope's beauty. She graciously accepted the compliments and thanked them both for their kind words.

Uncle Fly began the conversation by asking me if I knew anything about Columbian gold or red bud. All I knew was it was extremely expensive. At that time, the average pound of marijuana cost about one hundred and thirty dollar a pound. In contrast, a pound of Columbian would cost five hundred dollars a pound. He had a sample, but neither he nor Unck smoked weed. They wanted me to try it and give them my opinion of it. Hope spoke up, "Hey I smoke weed too!" Uncle Fly gave me a sample of both the red bud and the gold bud.

The Ojays had a new album out, and Uncle Fly had it already. He ripped the cellophane wrapping from its' cover and removed the album. He placed the album on the turntable and turned it on. Hope an d I were smoking the weed, and I totally understood why it cost so much. The flavor was unbelievable and had a fruity body aroma. You could almost swear you felt a rush with each toke.

The Ojays were singing, Let Me Make Love to You, and Hope was singing the words along with the record. When the song ended, Hope took my hand and said, "Come on." I didn't have a clue as to what she was talking about, and I let her know I was baffled. Then she came right out and asked. "Can I make love to you?"

I was caught off guard and was totally surprised by the question. I wasn't hitting on Hope. Hope was hitting on me! I picked her up and carried her to the bedroom Uncle Fly had told me was my very own. There was a bedroom set, and there were pink sheets on the bed. The walls were a mint green, and there were no curtains on the windows. The windows had old newspaper covering them. There was a lot of dust, but that was minor. The only thing this room really needed was a thorough cleaning.

I gently laid her across the bed and laid down beside her. I tried my best to savior every bit of the happiness I was experiencing at that moment. We began kissing, while we hurriedly took our clothes off. Hope was an amazing beauty. She had a slender build, but she was extremely shapely and curvy. I asked her if she were on birth control pills, and she became so sad she began tearing up.

"No." she answered. She then proceeded to try to kiss me, but something wasn't right. She was overwhelmed with grief, and I felt a need to comfort her. I did my best assure her that I was so impressed by her, there was nothing she could've told me that could change that. "I can't have children. If you want to have children, I will never be able to give you that. I know you want children. What man doesn't want children?" she blurted out.

"You have a little girl. Isn't she your daughter?" I asked. She told me the whole story about how she was shot in the stomach during a bank robbery attempt with Fat James. She had to get a hysterectomy. Not only was she left unable to have children, she also was eliminated from having to deal with a menstrual cycle. I remembered how attentive she had been towards her daughter, whenever I had seen them together. She was her only child, and she will forever be her only.

She searched my eyes to see how I felt about what I had learned. I was delighted! No periods meant I could have sex with her anytime I pleased. I loved the idea of no matter how many times I ejaculated while inside of her, she couldn't get pregnant. I thought It was a dream come true.

We resumed where we had left off, before it got too heavy, by kissing. Her tongue was sweet from all the candy she had been sucking on. She was so pretty, I often stopped just to stare at her.

Hope sat up just enough to get in a comfortable position and began sucking on my now fully erect penis. I looked into her eyes, and I could sense it was a special moment. She was letting me know she was submitting to me, and she did it by communicating with me using only her eyes. Once she knew I understood the moment, she went about doing her very best to please me. She closed her eyes and began to literally fuck my penis with her throat. She never flinched nor gaged. I knew she was trying to make me cum, when she pulled my penis from her throat, but left the head in her mouth. After clamping her lips down around base of the head, she began stroking the shaft between her thumb, and forefinger while looking deep into my eyes. It was as though she were both begging, yet at the same time, giving me permission to ejaculate in her mouth. I'd taken a hit of THC earlier. I was still under the influence of the hallucinogen; therefore, I was nowhere near ready for a climactic ending.

She had done such an amazing job orally, I felt obligated

to return the favor. I was eager to do my best, so I began by kissing and pulling gently on her nipples. I was moved to bite them lightly and to suck on them, as I gripped her breast in my huge hands.

After what seemed like a long time, I ran my fingers through her pubic hairs. She had a thick black bushy bush. Hairy vaginas were the norm back then, and Hope had the thickest bush I'd ever seen. I showered her body with kisses as I worked my way down. When I got to her belly button she stopped me by cupping my chin in her hand and shook her head. "Fuck me!" she whined.

I tried to get on top of her, but she motioned for me to lay on my back. She climbed on top of me and straddled my thighs. She took my penis in her fist and pumped it as hard and fast as she could, all awhile she rose up. Once she had risen high enough, she aimed my penis towards the opening of her moist vagina, and slowly lowered herself on it. As her vagina traveled down my shaft, I could feel her muscles massaging my penis by griping and releasing it, repeatedly.

She began to ride me. It was as though she had taken on the responsibility of making sure it was an enjoyable moment for the both of us. I allowed her to take the lead and ride me. I wanted to learn exactly how she liked to move, and how deeply or shallow she liked it. I was about to find out which rhythm she enjoyed the most, and so forth and so on

I concluded she liked it hard, fast and deep inside her. I eventually caught on to her rhythm and began to match her stroke for blessed stroke. There was something about the way she worked her vagina muscles that alerted me. I knew I would soon spill my semen if she continued to milk my penis with the muscles in her vagina. I tried my best to hold back, but the only way that would have been possible, would've been if I stopped matching her stroke for stroke, so I stopped to delay the climax.

She screamed in protest, "Don't stop! What are you doing? Why you stop!" I told her I stopped because I was getting ready to cum. "So was I!" she added with a groan of disappointment. I immediately resumed matching her stroke for stroke and turned her groans of disappointment into moans of gratifying pleasure. The break in the action allowed me to calm down my need to ejaculate. Even so, I still was only able to hold out for another five minutes, before I exploded inside of her. I ejaculated so hard and it felt so good I hadn't noticed she had collapsed atop of me. Her head laid beside mine.

"Thanks baby. I needed that." She whispered in my ear. I was surprised. I thought the fact that I came so quickly would have drove her away, but it didn't. Whereas Nett liked intercourse to last for at least forty-five minutes, Hope was the complete opposite. She wanted it to be extremely intense, but over quickly.

"I want to be with you Tone." she told me. I wondered how we could be anymore together than we already were, so I asked her. She began laughing, "I'm not talking about being with you like this silly. I want to be your woman and be with you all the time." Just like that, Hope became my woman and we became inseparable. Curt, Hope, and I had a new home, and a new beginning.

Chapter Twelve

Everyday Uncle Fly would show up during the early noon hour. Bigfoot would show up shortly thereafter. Bigfoot and Uncle Fly were also business partners. Bigfoot fought for the heavyweight title of the world. He lost but his share of the purse was one hundred thousand dollars. He invested his money in street drugs. Uncle Fly was in charge of the money and they both made a ton of loot using his connections. They were still making money long after the initial investment. Bigfoot was just as rich as Uncle Fly.

I hardly made any money on the first shipment it was gone so quickly. It took a couple of days just for me to learn the cliental, it was so huge. Uncle Fly promised me I'd make one hundred times the amount of money I made, on the next shipment. "When can we expect to get some more work?" I asked Uncle Fly.

He told me to watch the weather report on the news. "Whenever it rains in El Paso Texas, it rains over the Rio Grande River. The Mexicans would wait until it rained, and that's when they would take a chance on crossing the river with the work. A couple of days after that, the work arrives on our doorsteps."

I began to watch the news diligently. Of course, I paid special attention to the Meteorologist. There seemed to never be any mentioning of precipitation. I played with Curt and walked him about two or three times a day, just trying to keep busy. Every time I left the house Hope was dead on my heels. It didn't bother me at all. Whenever I got the car, we hung out as a loving couple.

I told Hope all about Marty, and she was very understanding. She told me it was the fact that I was honest that made it all acceptable. She told me she was already family oriented and was used to having wife in-laws. She then insisted upon meeting Marty. "I want to meet her today, if you don't mind." Since she made the request, as soon as we were in the car going to hang out, I headed to see Marty.

Marty was in her mother's house when I pulled up with Hope in the car. I parked next to Marty's car, and as I was getting out of the car, Marty stuck her head out the screen door. "Hey baby!" she yelled as she waved at me. She came out on the porch as Hope and I climb the stairs. She met me at the top of the stairs and slid right into my arms. Satisfied that I wasn't resisting her advances, she turned her attention towards Hope and asked, "Who's this?"

I introduced them, and informed Marty that Hope was my new girlfriend. I was very pleased as Marty took it upon herself, from that point on, to make Hope feel welcomed and at home. She took Hope to the side and had a talk. I don't have a clue as to what the conversation was about.

Marty's mother Biggum had been drinking and was demanding my attention. "Come in the kitchen and spend some time with yo momma." she said as she took my hand and led me to the kitchen table. She invited me to take a seat, before taking a seat herself.

"I need to know what's going on with you. I see you riding

around in a fancy car, with a fancy woman, and the first thing that comes to mind is you're not going back to school." I had to admit pursuing a degree was the very last thing on my mind at that time. I had such a bad experience with higher education, I concluded higher education wasn't for me. I tried my best to explain this to Biggum, but she would hear none of it. She insisted that I reconsidered my stance. "We need you to be a better role model son. If you dismiss getting your degree, and become a successful dope man, don't you realize how many of these kids, who idolize you, will try to emulate you? We don't need better pimps and drug dealers. We need dedicated men, who are determined to make a difference. What you're doing is much more harmful than you realize."

I thought about what she was saying, and I knew she was right. There was no way I could do anything without influencing all the youngsters who looked up to me, and there were quite a few. I knew at that very moment I had to return to school. I felt didn't have to return for myself. I had to do it for my family, and for my people.

Marty and Hope came into the kitchen and caught the tail end of the conversation. Marty was excited and offered her very own words of encouragement. She too admitted she had become concerned about me giving up on getting a degree. I looked around the room at all the concerned faces and made a promise to everyone I would seek out a school in New Port and continue to attend school until I've received a degree. Marty was so happy, she ran to my arms, and slid her tongue in my mouth. We shared a kiss just as passionate as the moment, and Hope was smiling from ear to ear the entire time. I don't know what was said during that conversation

Hope and Marty had, but we all seemed to be on the same page afterward.

We left there and went to the Hole. When we got there, I took Hope with me to the back room, and knocked on the door. Uncle Lucky answered the door, and you could tell by the expression on his face he had grown quite fond of me. "Where have you been Tone? He asked." I missed seeing you around."

"Hey Uncle Lucky!" I responded in kind as we entered the room. "I've just been trying to stay out of trouble." He studied my face to see if I was serious. As he looked me and Hope over, he appeared pleased by what he saw, and he commended me.

For some reason, I thought of Wendy, and wondered how she was doing. She really looked as though she were struggling to keep a grip on reality the last time I saw her. I asked Uncle Lucky if I could use the telephone behind the bar. The pay phone took coins, and I didn't feel like the hassle. He gave me a nod, and just as I was leaving, Easy asked me, "Who is this lovely young lady you're leaving back here with us?" I quickly introduced them and made my exit.

Kari brought the telephone to me. I called Slims' house trying to catch up with him, and Obie. It was the only way I knew of to check on her, without appearing to be checking on her. I was happy to hear Slims' voice when he answered. He told me Wendy had a serious mental breakdown one day when Obie took her to the track to work. They had to take her away in a straitjacket.

I instantly felt as though I had been kicked in the gut. My worst fear for her had become a reality. How cruel I thought it was to be taken advantage of and sexually exploited, the way everyone had done her. I asked about Obie, and how he was doing. I was not happy with the way he handled the situation, but he was still my little cousin, and I was concerned about him. A couple of days after Wendy's episode, Obie was pulled over by the police in Wendy's car. Wendy's people had reported the car stolen. After the police questioned him, he was released. He had since, moved back to his mother's house. I told Slim I was on my way to his house and hung up.

When Hope and I got in the car, she was excited, and extremely talkative. She also was as high as a witchdoctor! "Baby, them niggas got a lot of love and respect for you. They treated me like I was somebody special!" She stopped and looked around to make sure no one was listening to her and continued. "They said you're a stone, cold killer. Is it true you did time for murder when you were only sixteen?"

There it was. She had asked the question. I knew it would come up sooner or later, so I didn't lie. I told her the whole story, about how and why it all happened. I told her I really was digging her, and I'd hope it didn't make a difference between us.

She squealed with laughter, and told me, "Women love a man with a razor-sharp edge. You're dangerous Tone, and everybody knows that. It's because you've showed everybody how much I mean to you, that I now feel safe and protected. Now everybody knows if they mess with me, they'll have to deal with you, and believe me baby… everybody knows you don't play!"

We spent some time with Slim, and he told me he had decided to devote more time to pimping. I don't know what it was he was going through, or what it was that had him so shook up, but it seemed to have passed. He was his old self again. He was happy for me. He absolutely adored the car. It has been said, the Oldsmobile Toronado was the experimental car for the Eldorado. Pimps loved the Eldorado, so the Toronado was another pimp favorite. I promised him I would return with Hope, one day soon just too hang out.

The word was all over the hood that Hope was now my woman. All the fellas had tried to get with her, but it was me she chose to be with. My entire family met her, and began to love her, and that included all of my brothers and sisters, Unck, Auntie, and all of their children. One day while we were hanging out with Unck and Auntie watching the news, the news I had been waiting for was finally announced. There was a severe thunder storm taking place in El Paso, Texas. Unck had no idea why I was so excited, so I explained everything to him. Afterwards, Unck began spending time at the spot every single day. We were all waiting on the work to arrive and did it ever!

That is when I first met Chico. He was the biggest Mexican I'd ever met. He stood about six foot, four inches tall, and weighed well over two hundred and fifty pounds. He had backed his cargo van into the garage and opened its' rear doors. We all helped to unload the van and carry everything upstairs. Chico and I bonded during the short time, and looked forward to a more in-depth conversation, but he had to leave to go get the THC tablets first. Uncle Fly let us try some of the Columbian red bud and the gold bud. I must admit, they were both excellent. I preferred the red bud however, it was only a matter of taste.

A young girl about fourteen years old, arrived in a cab. She looked much older than fourteen, but she was in fact only fourteen. Uncle Fly immediately took her into the other bed room. Moments later, you could hear the bedsprings come to life singing a sexual squeaking song.

It wasn't the first young girl he had sex with in his room. There were seven different under aged girls who took turns showing up at the spot to have sex with Fly, every day of the week. Every one of them was extremely beautiful and looked much older than they were. The way they dressed and wore makeup, made it difficult to guess their ages. The only way I found out, was through conversations I had with them. He paid them three hundred dollars every time he had sex with them, and I witnessed no other function they fulfilled. He would use each one of them at least twice a week. Slowly the realization came to me, and I concluded Uncle Fly was one of those accepted pedophiles, as ridiculous as that may sound. It has always been as though pimps, entertainers and drug dealers were exempt from all the statutory rape laws, as well as the stigma usually associated with those labeled as pedophiles. A blind eye is turned, and children become fair pry, for certain predators.

Eventually the bed springs ceased to make noise. As the bed room door opened, they emerged totally nude. They were giggling and making a mad dash to the bathroom.

Bigfoot arrived, so Unck let him in. They sat on the sofa in the living room and busied themselves making arrangements for the expected onslaught of business activity. Hope and I were enjoying ourselves, as we went through an amazing album collection. We had already selected War's latest album entitled, Why Can't We Be Friends. We were listing to the track, Low Rider, when Chico finally returned. By that time, we were all in our own worlds.

Uncle Fly announced he was leaving to take the young

girl home, and he would return shortly. He counted out three hundred dollars in front of everyone and handed it to her. He took her by the hand and led her to the front door, all while she protested and begged to stay. He ignored her pleads and escorted her out the door.

When he came back, he had another young girl with him. Her name was Nene. She told me she was nineteen, and she had been Uncle Fly's girl for almost five years. Uncle Fly had brought her there to count the THC tablets. She had a system. She used a triple beam scale and weighed them by the thousands. We had a million tablets to count and pack.

I was eager to get started, however, it seemed Uncle Fly only had one thing on his mind. Off into the room he and Nene went. Hope and I looked at each other and burst into laughter. He had just finished with one young girl, and here he was about to get busy with another. When the bed began squeaking again, we all burst into laughter. Unck convinced Bigfoot to give him a ride home. "No use waiting around for him. He's gonna be a minute!" Unck said with a chuckle. "How's that old fart able to do all that fucking, anyway?" he wondered out loud.

Chico hung out with me for a while just kicking it about the business. He gave me a lot of information and insight about what to expect. He told me there was a million hits of THC to sort, and it takes all night just to remove all the broken ones and count only the good ones. He also informed me they were the best heroin connection in the Midwest. They had no distributors in Newport, and they had been unsuccessful at convincing Uncle Fly to at least recommend someone who would be interested in distribution. I believed this was confirmation that I was about to take my rightful position on top of Newport's heroin trade. According to Chico, all I had to do was convince Uncle Fly to wet his beak a bit, and the rest would take care of itself. The money in the heroin business is as addictive as the drug.

Hope asked me for permission to take advantage of a rare opportunity she had to spend the night with her daughter. Since I was going to be working all night, it was perfect. I had overlooked the fact that Hope was a mother. Because her daughter was not with us, sometimes it would simply slip my mind. I would never object to her spending time with her daughter.

Uncle Fly was a family man. He had a wife and five children, and he made sure to make it home every night by a decent hour. Even on this night he left me and Nene alone to handle the task at hand. Nene had done it so many times she was a seasoned veteran. It took her all of five minutes to teach me her technique, and we were off and running.

"You're gonna be up until this time tomorrow morning." he warned me. I need you to put five twenty-pound bricks in nine garbage bags. When I come back I will have some people with me. Break down one pound into ounces. Have it ready, because timing will be everything. Tomorrow is going to be a long day for you, but you'll make an awful lot of money. I promise you that." He waved as he left out the back door.

It took us all night to count and pack the THC tablet into packages containing one thousand hits apiece, just as had been predicted. While sorting through the tabs looking for the broken ones, we would swallow them if we felt sleep trying to come on. The others we put aside to take later. It also raised our level of concentration.

The next morning, I walked Curt early. I was expecting

to be busy, and I didn't want to get so busy I would have to ignore or neglect his needs. I fed him, and spent my remaining free time brushing him.

Uncle Fly was the first to arrive. He had a couple of white guys with him, and they wanted to purchase one hundred pounds. They agreed to pay five hundred dollars per pound, if it were indeed Columbian red bud. It was my responsibility to make sure they were able to sample the product. It meant helping them by fulfilling any request they may have had for what they considered necessary paraphernalia.

I was a salesman, but if the truth of the matter was told, their minds were already made up. They were anxious to buy, and the product was remarkable. So remarkable in fact, it actually sold itself. After the money had been counted, I assisted them in loading their pounds into a cargo van.

After they had left, Uncle Fly counted out two thousand five hundred dollars, and handed it to me. "You're guaranteed to make at least twenty-five thousand dollars on bud alone. I'm paying you twenty-five dollars for every pound you sell. The THC is where you'll make most of your money. I'm paying you five cents a hit."

If you didn't do the math, you'd be just as puzzled by the statement as I was, but it was true. I was going to make fifty thousand dollars off the tabs. The most beautiful thing about this whole set up, was Uncle Fly provided all the customers as well.

I spent the day meeting people, selling marijuana, and THC tabs. I sold the tabs for three hundred and ninety dollars per thousand. They sold for a dollar apiece on the streets, so a three hundred, and ninety, dollar investment would bring a profit of six hundred dollars.

It all was so unreal to me. By the end of the day, I had more money than I'd ever had at one time in my life! Uncle Fly warned me to save my money, and when spending make sure the purchase is for something worthwhile. He was giving a pool party at his home for the family soon. He was eager to show me the lifestyle money could provide, and the upcoming party would be the perfect opportunity. I was just as excited as he. I'd never been to a pool party in anyone's backyard before.

The next morning over breakfast Hope told me she was going to write Fat James a letter and let him know it was over. She expressed a desire to be my woman from now on. I felt it was all quite sudden. Maybe it was because she hadn't seen him in a while. It could have been because I didn't want to deal with qany of t the drama there would have been once he was released from prison, if they still had feelings for one another. I paid all the expenses for her to go visit him, and have the opportunity resolve their issues face to face.

When Hope came home, she told me the visit helped her realize it wasn't because she had been apart from James that made her feel the way she did about me. She told me she loved me and said that's exactly what she told Fat James. She also told him she wouldn't be back to visit again. I loved Hope, and for the first time in my life I had found someone who truly needed me and was with me to face whatever life had in store for us. I wasn't alone anymore.

Fat James wrote me a letter telling me we all must think he has life! He threatened to kill me upon his release from prison. I was furious and deeply offended by the letter. According to the rules of the game, the woman did the choosing. You can't get upset or start a beef with someone just because your woman chooses another. I wrote a reply to his letter. In the letter I stated how I understood how losing his freedom, and his woman may have also made him lose his common sense. I informed him I would over look his indiscretion this time, but he should keep in mind the type of individual I am. I would be at the bus station with my pistol waiting to greet him. I promised him I would settle the dispute before it even had a chance to become a conflict. Since I had given him a shot at convincing Hope to stay down with him, I'd hoped he would accept the fact his woman wanted me.

I was so happy Hope was back, and it was perfect timing. It was the day of the pool party. Uncle Fly came to pick us up to take us to the party. By the time we arrived the party was in full swing. Everybody I thought would be there, was already there! Unck and Auntie, where in the pool with Herman, Pam, and Spencer.

The house was amazing! It was huge, and was clearly the largest and most beautiful house I'd ever been guest in. As we were walking into the pool area, Fly's oldest son was diving from an upstairs balcony into the Olympic size pool. It was such a magnificent dive, you could tell it wasn't his first time attempting it.

Ben was Unck's youngest son. He struggled to lead as normal a life as possible with cerebral palsy. His mind was sharp, but his speech was slurred, and he could barely walk, even with assistance. He was my little brother, and he was extremely proud of that fact. I would always help him walk, or I carried him. I sensed he didn't have long before he wouldn't be able to walk, so I did my best to help him to walk, as much as possible. When he was no longer able to walk, I wanted him to have plenty of memories of walking to reflect upon. I loved him from the very first time I spent time with him.

Uncle Fly introduced me to his wife, Francine. She was a tall, thick, strikingly beautiful woman. She had an inviting yet, tough persona. It was easy to see she oversaw everything going on, as she continuously gave instructions to the busy staff. She offered praise, and reprimands on the fly, as the situation called for.

She asked out loud, "Is this your girl?" as she nodded her head in Hope's direction. I'd learned a long time ago how important first impressions are. I didn't want to come across as foolishly, and hopelessly in love just yet. I just couldn't be the cool unaffected guy, with the gorgeous woman on my side that I wanted to be, no matter how hard I tried. I was beaming with pride, and couldn't hide that fact, no matter how hard I tried. I admitted the lovely young woman I was escorting, was indeed my woman. She squealed with delight as she announced, "You two will be the hit of this party! You're such a handsome couple!"

She inquired if we had swimsuits or not. We didn't come to the pool party to swim. Neither of us even owned a suite. Francine insisted we wear swimsuits, so we could show off our bodies. She told us we'd be eye candy for her guest, and that would go a long way to help make her party a huge success. She led us to her finished basement, where she stored the swimsuits. She was always being followed by her close friends. Every step she took, they appeared to be right on her heels. She picked out six or seven suits and handed them to Hope. Then she instructed her friends to show Hope the master bedroom's bathroom, and to assist her in picking out the suite that showed off her curves the best.

I thought it was a very kind gesture until I took notice, we were in the basement alone. She handed me about five different pair of swim trunks and told me to try on every one of them, so she could decide which pair I would wear. "Where's the bathroom?" I asked, as I looked around at the many doors that could have been one.

"I've seen more than my share of dicks." She answered. "Let me see what's so impressive about yours. The print of your crotch is both inviting and promising." I was surprised she was so blunt. She made me want to flaunt myself in front of her. It was unlike any experience I'd ever had. The fact that someone could come in and catch us at any given moment, enhanced our sexual drive which already was in full effect.

"I want to see it hard." She said before she reached out and began stroking me. As crazy as I was about Hope, it didn't matter. My penis had no conscience. She had barely touched me, before my penis seemed to spring into a full erection. She made a few raunchier comments, while she had her eyes closed. All the while, she was stroking me. "We're going to have so much fun this summer!" she whispered. "Now get dressed."

I put on the swim trunks she had selected for me to wear, then we went back upstairs and into the family room. She had bragged to me about her extensive album collection, which she kept in the family room. I selected the Isley Brother's latest album entitled, The Heat is on, and threw it on the turntable. By this time, she had told me to call her Aunt Francine. It wasn't because she wanted to be like an aunt to me. She said she wanted everyone to believe we had that type of a relationship, so we could spend time together without drawing suspicion. She then selected the album, Romantic Warrior, by Return to Forever, and added it to the turntable.

We continued until we had made enough selections to serve as the soundtrack for the party. Our main objective when selecting an album was, the entire album could be played, and not just certain selections. There were quite a few recording artists who were able to produce such a desirable product during those days. It was an enjoyable chore someone had to do. Besides, there was no better of an opportunity to check out a well put together album collection. The music we selected blared through the huge speakers in the backyard.

Hope came down the stairs dressed in a yellow bikini. She was an absolute knock out! What was most exciting to me, was the way she was looking at me. She looked at me as though I was the best-looking man she'd ever seen in her life. She ran to me and embraced me. "Damn you look good!" she yelled with no shame. Then she kissed me hard and deeply. Aunt Francine interrupted us by simply clearing her throat. "Come on you two. There will be plenty of time for all of that later, but for now, there's a whole crowd of people out there just waiting for ya'll to dazzle em!"

She took me by my hand and led us through the double doors of solid oak. The doors opened up to a patio near the pool. Uncle Fly was stretched out on a lawn chair, surrounded by some of Newport's most known gangsters. They all were dressed in swim shorts and stretched out on lawn chairs. Uncle Fly Gordon, Sidewalk Slim, Red Top, and Mad Dog, were all engaged in a heavy discussion.

Auntie and Pam yelled for Hope to join them near the grill, where they were enjoying some barbeque ribs. There was an empty chair next to Uncle Fly, and he gently patted the seat of the chair with hand. I took it as an indication he wanted me to take a seat, so I sat down. After which Aunt Francine quickly brought me a tall cold glass of Brass Monkey on the rocks, a lit joint, then just as quickly as she had appeared, she departed.

Uncle Fly raised his glass and announced, "To our long lost, nephew!" Everyone followed suit and raised their glasses in my direction and saluted me. I in turn raised my glass to acknowledge the gesture, along with a nod. I felt as though I had just been through some sort of initiation into a secret society. I raised the glass to my mouth and took a drink. Everyone else did the same.

The business discussions began! They were a tightknit organization, and as a group they laid out my responsibilities to me. They also explained why I was expected to carry myself in a certain manner, so I would not bring shame upon the organization.

The organization was nameless. However, its' members were all very well known. Everyone was required to be able to stand on their own, with a solid street reputation. I was the youngest, but my name was ringing more like the liberty bell its' self, announcing the arrival of a true rebel. I was already known as a killer, having served time for murder at the tender age of sixteen. Lately I'd been recognized as a very good street hustler. I had never felt so honored and accepted than I did at that moment. I felt I truly had arrived. I was a Dopeman!

Chapter Thirteen

Things were going great! I was making unbelievable amounts of money, and Hope proved to be a solid woman and lover. As far as Uncle Fly was concerned, we were doing great. Unfortunately, I begged to differ. I felt it was time for Uncle Fly to step up his game and get in the heroin trade like everybody else was doing. We had several conversations on the subject, and I tried my best to convince him we could rule the city with a connection as solid as his.

There was a huge international bust, whereas the French connection went down, and so did China white heroin. Mexican mud was ushered in almost immediately, along with a new normal. Mexican mud wasn't even ten percent as strong as China white, so the profit margin was affected dramatically. What an addict had once purchase for one dollar, now cost ten dollars. It was an adjustment that was taking place, and the Mexicans became the new controllers of the market. It was imperative for me to convince Uncle Fly that I knew the game quite well and could handle things.

I explained to him that Mexican mud was brown, like the color of coffee. Although the mud couldn't take nearly as much of a cut as the China white was able to, there still was a huge potential for monetary gain. I once witnessed someone take one once of China white heroin and turn it into a whole kilo using cut. Even then, it was still too strong to put on the streets. The most I've ever seen an ounce of Mexican mud cut, and still was too strong for the streets, was to turn it into two ounces. There still were tremendous amounts of money, just waiting to be claimed.

As it turned out, I wasn't the only one trying to convince Uncle Fly to consider the heroin trade. All the other partners, and the connection itself, began leaning on him. Uncle Fly resisted the change, because he didn't have a heroin cliental, and the healthy respect he had for the Mexican gangsters he dealt with. He oversaw the market he took part in, and if anything went wrong, he still felt a sense of control. He would have to trust someone with his very life, because if anything went wrong, the price could very well be his life as retribution. It all depended on the transgression, and the details of the offense.

One day Uncle Fly showed up at the spot and handed me an ounce of heroin. I thought it was a declaration of the confidence he had in me. I was disappointed because its' color was beige. I knew enough to know the color was an indication the stuff had already been cut. I was going to have to sell it on the streets by the bags to get rid of it, it had so much cut on it. "Uncle Fly!" I protested. "Somebody done pulled some bullshit! This shit has already been cut."

"No, it hasn't." he insisted. "I gave it to you just like I got it. Can you do anything with it?" he asked. I had to explain to him, it was because it had been --cut we had no idea how strong or how weak it was. I would have to take some of it, to get it tested. "Take my car. I'll be here when you get back."

I hopped in the car and headed to see Uncle Lucky. He had a lot of junkie friends who would tell him the truth about the potency of some heroin. When I had initially shown him the product, he said exactly what I had concluded. "This has already been stepped on, Tone." He had a puzzled expression on his face before asking. What is this supposed to be?" I told uncle Lucky I believed it had been diluted also, but I needed to know how strong, or how weak it was.

He went to the front door of the bar and called out to Skillet. Skillet was a heroin addict who hung out around the bar doing odd jobs and running errands for hits. He was a very small man, but you couldn't tell if he were petite or malnourished. We measured out two McDonalds spoons, and gave them to Skillet to check out. We waited while he went across the street to his girlfriend's house to inject sample.

Hope went to the juke box, and played Harold Melvin and the Blue Noes tune entitled, Bad Luck. I remember thinking, and hoping it wasn't an omen. It wasn't long before Skillet returned with the great news.

"Man, it's really good." I asked him how much I would be able to put on it, and his answer confirmed all my suspicions. "It's already been cut. It's better than anything else around right now, but if you cut it anymore it won't be as good as the rest of the shit that's around.

My spirit was floored by the disappointment. My breath was shortened, and my heart fluttered. The news couldn't have been more devastating or disappointing. There was no way this would make us competitive with the rest of the big boys in the market. Uncle Fly appeared to be trying to work me, but it didn't add up. He knew nothing about the game, and I knew his connection didn't give it to him like that. I smelled a rat. Who cut the dope was the haunting question to me? I also wondered why.

I still had the ounce to sell, but there was a problem. It had been cut so much I would have to sell ten-dollar bags directly to the addicts on the streets, to get rid of it. I left the bar with my head down, and my shoulders slumped. Hope grabbed my arm as we were walking back to the car, and whispered in my ear, "Pick your head up Baby. Never let them see you down. It's a damn shame, but our people feed off that kind of shit. You're a bad muthafucka Tone!" She stopped walking and got in my face to make sure she had my undivided attention. "You'll make whatever has to work, work!"

As I looked into her smiling, believing eyes, I felt a surge power. All the self-doubt that was attempting to creep into my subconscious, was nipped in the bud. I wondered how she knew I needed to hear those words. I returned her smile, and we headed to the car. I had to talk to Uncle Fly, but I also had to check on my brother.

The fall season was upon us, and the leaves had already changed colors. The air was crisp, and had a slight chill carried by a gentle breeze. Which was a clear indication the weather would be changing, and soon we would be needing sweaters and jackets.

When we arrived at Albert's house, you could smell the marijuana being smoked in the house all the way to the sidewalk! One of the reasons Uncle Fly agreed to try the heroin trade was because of a deal we made. He was afraid if I got involved in the heroin trade, I would switch completely over to heroin, and make a career out of it. There's a long list of black men who have gained notoriety simply by getting the right drug connection. The streets of our communities get polluted with drugs, and our brothers and sisters end up either incarcerated or even murdered if a deal or robbery goes bad.

"If I do this, and I'm saying if because my mind is telling me I'm doing the wrong thing. The only way I'll do this, is if you return to school and maintain at least a three, point zero grade point average. You're too bright to end up being just another street nigga. You're gonna play a major role in destroying a lot of lives. I hope once you get your degree, you'll be smart enough and rich enough to get out of the game. Remember to try to repair some of the damage we are sure to cause."

I agreed, so now it was my plan to convince Albert to go to school with me. When we entered my brother's house without knocking. We found Albert sitting at the dinning-room table wearing a huge smile. There were three pairs of Swedish knit pants on the table, and Albert was excited. "Hey bro! I found a hookup where we can get Swedish knit pants for ten dollars a pair." It was an amazing deal! Swedish knit pants were sixty dollars a pair in the stores.

"How many pair can we buy?" I inquired. He told me we could purchase as many pairs as we could afford, and they came in all sizes, colors, and styles. "I'm gonna buy twenty pairs. Ten for you and ten for me. I want you to go back to school with me, so we'll need some school clothes anyway. He gave me a puzzled look, so I explained it all to him. He asked me what school I was thinking about attending. "Jochannan College at Newport." was my answer.

"Man, Jochanna has a hell of a basketball team. You should try out for the team." He said as he was beginning to warm up to the idea about going back to school. Jochanna was the only all black college in the state. It wasn't an historical black college yet, but well on its' way to becoming one. "This is your chance to get into the pros!" Albert seemed to be gazing through a window into the future, as he uttered the words.

Suddenly, and unexpectedly, I thought of Tri City. The heroin in Tri City couldn't be as strong as the heroin in Newport. I believed I could go there and get rid of the ounce I had. It would be easy to sell, so I asked my brother if he would take me there, so I could sell it. I trusted my brother more than I trusted anyone. No matter what went on in our lives, there were no people who loved me more, or whom I trusted more than my family. He agreed to make the road trip with me.

Of course. Hope protested once she realized she wasn't included in my plans. "You ain't going nowhere without me, Tone. You can throw that bullshit out your mind if that's what you're thinking." She had her hands on her hips and was glaring at me as though she was ready to fight to stand her ground. It was because of her insistence that I reluctantly caved in to something other than my better judgment.

"Okay, all I'll have to do is find out what Uncle Fly wants for this, and we can be on our way tomorrow." We had a plan. I would be able to get rid of what I had, while concentrating on who cut the drugs and why. Since the drugs were cut out of my presence, it was obvious someone wanted to get a cut off my work before me!

Uncle Fly refused to give me a price for the once. "I just want to see what type of money could be made." was all the information I was able to get. It all was quite frustrating, and confusing. Why couldn't I get a straight answer about the price? Uncle Fly still insisted the drugs were uncut, in spite of my repeated objections. I still had to go to Tri City, to try to get the most I could out of the diluted product.

When we arrived in Tri City, all sorts of memories flooded my mind. I had once been one of the most popular kids in the city, and because of that, I was very fond of the Tri City. I even graduated from high school there. Everything was as clean, simple, and peaceful as I'd remembered. The leaves on the trees were demanding attention with its' brilliant display of beautiful bright fall colors. Even the fallen leaves that carpeted the ground, added to the beauty and peacefulness of the environment.

I had called Joe to let him know we were leaving, and what time to expect us. It was just a precautionary measure I took, since we were riding dirty. The ride there was uneventful. We arrived safely, and as we pulled into Joe's parent's driveway, you could see Joe on the porch waving. He had a huge smile on his face, and it was obvious he had timed our arrival perfectly.

I called Joe's father Uncle Joe, and his mother Aunt Irene. His father loved me just like an uncle, even though he knew my history. I loved my Aunt Irene. She was the type of woman who wore her heart on her sleeve. You didn't have to wonder if she liked you or not, because she'll find a way to let you know. She loved me deeply. She made no secret of the fact she didn't like my past nor my lifestyle, and despite my manners, politeness, and respectfulness, she was not fooled one little bit. She knew I lived by the code of the streets, and I was extremely danger.

We got out of the car, and I introduced everybody. After the exchange of warm, pleasant greetings, all the way around, we entered the house to offer our greetings and respect.

Aunt Irene was a very beautiful woman, who looked half

her age. She was petite, shapely, and her high cheekbones made her appear to have strong Indian features. She always had a serious expression on her face, and you knew instantly, she was the type of lady that didn't put up with any foolishness whatsoever. I was greeted by one of her rare vintage smiles, and a hug, which always warmed my heart. It used to make me feel so special to actually see her facial expressions change whenever she saw me.

She liked Hope right off and complimented her beauty. Uncle Joe was a big man, who wore a medium size afro hairdo and a full beard. We were involved in small talk and exchanging opinions on current events, when Aunt Irene made a gesture indicating she wanted me to follow her into the kitchen.

Once we were in the kitchen, she whispered in a very low and soft voice. "You know I can't allow you and your girlfriend to sleep together under my roof, right? I still have the girls living here, and it wouldn't be proper since ya'll ain't married." She studied my eyes for any sign of pain, and she must have seen what she was searching for. She apologized and begged me to understand her position. "I know you weren't expecting this expense, so I'll give you the money for a hotel room.

The gesture moved me, as well as warmed my heart. It truly made me feel special.

"That's not necessary, Aunt Irene. I have my own money, and I understand you are trying to raise lades." I hoped she didn't feel bad, and to make sure she knew I had no ill feelings I gave her a big hug. She exhaled as she hugged me back, and I sensed some to raise weight being lifted off her shoulders. She was relived not to be considered the heavy in the situation.

Then she shewed me out of her way, with a promise of mountains of buttermilk pancakes!

Once we had checked in and situated our luggage, I sat Joe down and got a rundown on the heroin trade in Tri City. I needed to know the players, and what was the highest level of potency on the streets. I knew Joe wouldn't know the answers to most of the questions, but whatever information he provided potentially could point me to the right people with the answers I sought.

I was delighted when Joe informed me the Raff family had Tri City's heroin market all bottled up. I insisted he take me directly to their location immediately. Their spot wasn't far from where we were. I also insisted upon Hope and Albert remaining behind, as I weighed out a gram. It wasn't a suggestion, nor was it a request. I had issued an order. I had never been to the spot, so I had no idea what to expect. Joe told me the spot also served as a shooting gallery. I didn't want to get caught in a compromising position or situation with my brother and my woman caught in the middle.

We arrived at well-kept yellow house, which had a single long white staircase in the rear. The stairs lead to a single door. It was an upstairs flat, and the entrance was in the kitchen. Robert and Clifford were the only family members there. Clifford was a young, tall, handsome brother. He was very ambitious and wanted a place in the affairs of the money makers and to be counted among those who made the decisions.

Robert on the other hand, was a free spirit, and happy just being a loose cannon. He hated stupidity and attacked it vigorously whenever he encountered it. Most found his huge personality intimidating. Unlike his brothers he was short, and there may have been a little Napoleon complex going on, however, there was nothing about the man that would lead you to believe he was anything other than a secure individual.

Robert and Clifford were first cousins, and running the place that day was their responsibility. There were a couple of guys sitting at the kitchen table injecting heroin into their veins. I explained to Clifford and Robert exactly what it was I was trying to do and showed them a gram I had weighed out before I left the hotel room.

Robert got so excited he couldn't contain himself. "That shit looks exactly like what we're selling." He looked at Clifford to confirm what he was saying, and Clifford nodded in agreement. Then he added, "And we have the best shit around here!" Clifford was beginning to get excited when he realized he and Robert were the only ones who knew what I had. Clifford informed us he had talked to his brother Charles earlier that morning, and he and Tommy should be in route to the spot as we spoke.

There was a green curtain hanging over the kitchen door. It served as a divider by separating the kitchen from the rest of the house. The kitchen was painted yellow and was spotless. You could see there was a lot effort and pride put into the cleaning and the running of this spot. You could smell the bleach and other cleaning ingredients in the air, and although I was in a shooting gallery, I was quite comfortable.

Suddenly the very popular Soul Train theme song, which is played at the beginning of every single program, could be heard blaring on a television set from behind the green curtain. As Don Cornelius was inviting everyone to join him on the hippest trip in America, Tommy and Charles walked through the door. The other two fellas who were now finished injecting their drugs, were escorted out.

Tommy was a tall, handsome fella. He also was a very sharp dresser. He wore a very expensive brown leather suite, with a matching hat. Charles was also a tall brother, and you could tell he considered himself a pretty boy. Between the two, you'd have to be blind not to recognize Tommy was a very serious businessman, whereas Charles intentions seemed more intended on impressing the ladies than getting rich. It was hard to take Charles seriously, but it was a mistake to deal with Tommy in any other manner.

"This is Tone. He's the dude from Newport I've been telling you about." Joe said speaking directly to Tommy. He smiled broadly and stuck out his hand. I gladly accepted the offer and took his hand into my own. We gave each other the popular black power handshake. It was a show of solidarity right from the beginning. We were rebelling against everything that had been forced upon us by the establishment as culture and customary tradition. The conventional handshake was one of the first things to go. I was so genuinely happy to meet him, and I could tell the feelings were mutual.

He asked me right off the top, "How much you gonna charge me for an ounce?" I felt compelled to be honest, but I couldn't reveal I wasn't given that information. I also didn't want to quote a wrong price. I've seen situations where pride prevented a deal from being made, simply because someone had spoken without the authority to do so. Most of the time it was not an issue, but if the buyer wanted to be difficult and insist upon the quoted price, it could cause egos to collide.

"I'm only here to see if there's a market for our product." The way I explained it, prices hadn't been set on anything yet. I was just feeling things out. I needed to see what type of market could be developed, based upon the strength of the heroin we had. We'll work the details out later, but for now all I brought with me was an ounce to see how much interest would be generated.

"Well let me see what you got lil bro." When Tommy laid eyes on the product his shoulders slumped, and you could see, as well as sense, his disappointment. "Man, this shit already done been stepped on. I need raw! Right now, I must drive all the way to Chicago to cop raw, but if I could have it delivered, I'd rather do that. It would eliminate the risk I take every time I hit the road dirty, but the shit must be raw and good to make it worth my while.

I assured him I could get it raw, but suggested we do a test to compare the two. Robert used heroin, so we had Robert inject two McDonalds' spoons of my drugs to get his opinion. McDonald's used to give away their specialty made spoons, which were made to stir their coffee. However, the spoons were the perfect size to measure out an approximate tenth of a gram. They became so popular among drug dealers they were named mac spoons, and law enforcement considered them drug paraphernalia. McDonalds discontinued having the spoons manufactured in a show of cooperation with law enforcement in their war on drugs. They came up with a new design. The coffee stirrer was no longer shaped like a miniature spoon therefore, it was rendered useless.

As soon as Robert injected the drug, he instantly went into a serious nod. He could no longer hold his head up. He was completely incoherent. I rationalized the situation and decided to use myself as a test subject. I could get no straight answers from Uncle Fly, Unck, and now Robert was unable to provide me with any input.

I wasn't worried about waking up the monster inside of me. I knew I was gambling with my life, and there was a very strong possibility the taste I had once developed for the drug could be awaken. It was a gamble I considered worth the calculated risk. The information I would receive would be first hand, and therefore invaluable.

I ordered a syringe and a dime bag of their stuff. There were a few big eyes as Clifford served me, and I took a seat at the kitchen table across from Robert. I looked at Robert and remembered what I had observed when the other guys had injected the drugs earlier. The difference was much more than obvious.

I told everyone that I had not used any heroin in about five years, therefore, any amount of the drug introduced to my system should render me into an unconscious state. Clifford asked me if I needed a tie, but I rejected the offer. I rolled up one of my sleeves and exposed my bulging veins. The needle easily pierced a vein. That was quite evident by the warmth from the blood causing condensation to form droplets as well as a slight mist, as the blood rushed into the syringe. I slowly pushed the brown liquid into my vein. I felt only a mild sensation as the drug slowly took effect. It was very mild rush, and I barely felt the effects of the drug at all, but it left you feeling like you were about to feel much more. I should have been plastered to the floor, but I barely felt it.

I had learned all there was to know about the drug everyone claimed was the best in the city. Now it was time for me to have some idea of what it was I was selling. I immediately took out my own drugs and measured out one mac. I refilled the syringe, but this time as I slowly pushed the brown liquid into my vein, I instantly felt the warmth and a strong taste of vinegar hit my stomach. I had only done half of the amount I had done of theirs. I felt like I had been launched into a blissful dream like state. The rush was amazing! Everything I had felt lead me to conclude there was no comparison. It was undoubtable that my drugs were the superior product.

"I just copped what I've got." Tommy explained. "If you can wait until I move what I have left, you can sell your shit right here. Then once you're finished, you can make a trip to fill my order. It has to be raw though, and I'll take a quarter of a key every week like clockwork."

There was a problem. I had to return to Newport in a couple of days. I informed him of my situation and added, "I'll just have to move what I can on the streets and get back with you next weekend." Tommy studied my face for a moment, then he looked at Robert, who was still in a deep nod. Robert held a burning cigarette between his fingers with an ash so long, it appeared as though the slightest movement would have caused it to break and fall to the floor. Tommy smiled, yet you could sense he was trying to conceal his excitement. We had forged a deal and sealed it with a firm handshake.

I had mixed emotions as we left the spot. I was happy because I knew if Uncle Fly would stop playing games, and produce the heroin in its' pure form, we would have both Tri City as well as Newport sewed up. On the other hand, I was faced with the dilemma of selling the drugs I had. I had nothing that even resembled a cliental.

Before we got to the car, Robert caught up to us. "Man, that shit is the bomb! You know why they want to sell their shit first right?" he asked. I hunched my shoulders and shook my head. I truly didn't have a clue. I thought mine was the better product, and it should've been used to draw the addicts. Robert reminded me, the family already owned a monopoly in the heroin trade. There was no need to attract addicts, because they were already coming.

"Their problem is making sure they get rid of their stuff, before anyone gets a taste of your shit. Once anyone gets a taste of what you have, ain't nobody gonna want that weak-ass shit, they got. They'll be stuck with it and have to take a lost. Depending on how often you plan on coming through."

I looked at Joe, and he had a faraway look in his eyes. I could tell he was thinking of something. He eventually spoke, "That dope fiend ass Pee Wee can sell that shit! Everybody fucks with that nigga."

Before I was able to answer, Robert spoke up, "Shit! I could sell it muthafucken myself. The family ain't treating me right because I'm using, but I could run this whole operation by myself." I gave his proposal some consideration. While I was thinking he interrupted my thoughts with a last-minute pitch.

"What have you got to lose? All you have to do is try me." I was thinking of the few options before me, and none of them assure me of being able to move all of my product within a couple of days. Robert continued, "Just pack up some dime bags, in bundles of twelve. Two would be mine, and ten will be yours. That way, I will make twenty dollars every time I sell twelve." I gave it some thought and decided to give it a try. Like he had pointed out so eloquently, he was my best option. We headed back to the room where I had left everything I needed to hook up the bags.

Upon entering the room, I immediately introduced

Robert to my brother and woman. Once the introductions were out of the way, I went about making up the packs of heroin. I used a notebook pad provided by the hotel to make small makeshift envelopes, to pack the drugs into. It all was done with a sense of urgency, but carefully done, to avoid any unnecessary problems. He told me to give him a couple of hours and struck out. It was more than obvious he was a man on a mission.

After he left, I explained the situation to Hope and Albert. I shared my plan with them. I told them it would be better if they went back to Newport without me. I had planned to leave in a couple of days, but that proved to be a miscalculation. It was going to take more than a couple of days to move a whole ounce. I didn't have access to the cliental I'd hoped for, so I had to put in some serious work myself.

Chapter Fourteen

I have never tried to hide anything I did out of shame, but I didn't tell Albert, or Hope I had injected heroin. I didn't want to give what I thought to be a reasonable explanation, nor did I want to allow them an opportunity to rebuttal or to give me an opinion. I did it because I wanted to. It was impossible to conceal the fact I intoxicated on heroin, so I never tried. I had no-one I had to answer to about any decisions I made. I was my own man.

I was feeling nauseous, and I knew some marijuana would make me feel better. Joe told me Bird Raff had some of the best weed he'd ever smoked. "It's called Columbian gold." That was all I needed to hear. Columbian red bud was my favorite, but my second choice would have been the gold bud. We left the room headed to get some buds from Bird.

I met Bird at a high school track meet where we were both competing. He wore sunglasses throughout the entire meet. I thought it was one of the coolest, most original things I'd ever witnessed. We talked a little that day, but neither of us knew at that time we would become as close as we were. It was because of my connection with the Raff family we were able to form a solid friendship.

We were more than thrilled to be reunited. We talked for about forty-five minutes, just catching up! The last time

I had talked to him, he lived in Albion. He had since moved to Tri City. I asked him why he wasn't involved in the heroin business with his family, and his response was, "That lifestyle only leads to trouble. I have a good woman and a wonderful son. I want to provide them with a safe and wholesome environment to thrive in. Who can argue with me about that?" I was happy for him and brought a lid of marijuana from him. A lid approximated would be about a half an ounce. We made promises to stay in touch, but we never saw each other again.

We left and went to the park across the street from the Dairy Queen. Hope and I were sitting on a park bench sharing a joint when Hope looked deeply into my eyes and said, "Baby I don't like the idea of leaving you here all alone. I hate that you've started using dope too." I knew what she was saying was the only logical conclusion anyone with a sound mind could come up with.

I tried my best to ease her worried mind. She had every right to be concerned. "Don't worry Hope. I'm through with that shit. I haven't done that shit in years, and I won't be doing it again. I promise you. It was not an enjoyable experience." She gazed into my eyes as though she were searching my soul for answers. Once she realized how ill I was, she began to feel bad for me. She flashed a forced shaky smile and kissed me. I kissed her back passionately. Neither one of us knew it would be the last time we shared such a loving kiss.

We all walked across the street to the Dairy Queen and ordered banana splits. While we were sitting there enjoying our ice cream, Robert pulled up on us in a gold Cadillac Coup Deville. He didn't get out the car. He simply waved for me to come over to the car. When I got there, he handed me one hundred dollars, and stated proudly, "I'm done. I need some more. Things are beginning to pick up as the word gets out about how good this shit from Newport is."

We all went back to the room and I put another bundle of twelve, ten-dollar bags For Robert. "They love this shit! I'll have all this shit sold in a couple of days." he was happy to report. Hope suggested we all stay and leave together, if it was truly indeed going to take only a couple of more day. I agreed with Hope and the matter was settled. I walked Robert to the door and let him out.

Afterwards I turned to Joe and told him to introduce me to Pee Wee. I believed if we had both Pee Wee and Robert soliciting, we would surely be able to move the ounce within a couple of days. I'm sure it wasn't what Robert had in mind. His desire was to be exclusive. He was helping me to establish a foundation for a cliental which would be completely independent of his family's business. He would become my righthand-man, thereby forcing his family to deal with him differently. He would be his family's connection. They would have to recognize him for the powerful position he would be in.

He may feel a little too threatened for there to be another connection his family could turn to. They may avoid dealing with him if another source was available. I'll simply inform him that I'm only using Pee Wee to sell what I have. After everything had been sol d, Pee Wee would have to get everything he needed from him.

Joe informed me that Pee Wee always hung out by the store begging for pocket change and looking for work about that time of day. When he said work, he was talking about dope to sell. He suggested we leave right then and try to catch him. "He should be really sick right now, and in need of some medicine." Joe added.

We all left the room together, and road with Joe. Before we left, I made up another bundle of twelve dime packs. I also made up an extra dime pack for Pee Wee to test. This test wasn't for me, but for Pee Wee. He would know the caliber of heroin he was dealing with, and his sickness would be taken care of, all at once. I wanted to be prepared, in case we located him.

Joe was right. We found Pee Wee in front of the store begging every single costumer, he could get to listen to him, for pocket change. He spared no one. He even hit up a couple small children for some pocket change! He needed a fix, and it showed. He was displaying all the signs. His nose was running. He hugged himself and trembled as though he felt a chill in the air. There was a sense of urgency in his mannerism. All the signs of desperation were in his wide eyes.

As I was getting out of the car we made eye contact and he called out my name. Tri City was a small city, and news traveled within the city limits quickly. "Give a nigga some work Tone!" he asked as I approached him.

"Oh, you already know my name!" I quickly retorted. "I was just about to have Joe introduce us, but I see that won't be necessary." He told me he remembered me from my high school days. He also informed me that the word on the streets was I had the best boy that city had seen in years. He said he had run into Robert earlier, and he had been informed about how excellent the product was.

I gave him the extra bag I had made up for him to try. I wanted him to be aware of just what it was he was dealing with. It was the top shelf. A heroin addict always works better after they've had their fix. If he were sick, all he would be able to concentrate on would be getting a hit. I knew from experience his decision making would be rooted in a strong desire to feed the beast within him.

I told him I would wait while he tried it out and give me his opinion. While he headed for the projects to handle his business I sat in the car reminiscing about the last time I was at that store. I met Wendy there, and all the memories made me daydream about all the great times we shared. I was wondering how she was doing, when a light tap on the window interrupted my thoughts.

It was Pee Wee, and it was obvious he was feeling no pain at all. He scratched the side of his face, as he struggled to keep his eyes open. He appeared to be fighting sleep to stay awake. When our eyes met, he managed to flash a broad smile. "Man, that's the best shit I've ever had." He managed to say with slurred speech. I began to wonder if I should put a cut on it myself, but I quickly dismissed the thought. I was pressed for time, and the sooner I finished the sooner I'll have an opportunity to convince Uncle Fly to produce the uncut product I was almost certain he had in his possession.

I handed Pee Wee the package and explained to him that the proceeds from ten packs were mine and the two were his. I then made him assure me he was satisfied with the arrangements. I got out the car and placed my arm around his shoulders. "Let's walk and talk." I said to him.

"I like you already Pee Wee, because game recognizes game. We can make a whole lot of money together. I'm also telling you right now, not to fuck up my money. If you do, I promise you I will not sleep under the same sky with you without hunting for you."

"Aww, you don't have to worry about no shit like that!" he said. I shook his hand and held it tightly. Refusing to release his hand, I held the firm grip until he looked into my eyes wondering what was going on. I've been told the eyes are the windows to the soul. I wanted him to take a good look, and see I meant what I was saying from the bottom of my heart. I then released his hand, turned my back on him, and walked to the car without even so much as a glance back.

After riding around smoking weed, we had developed a humungous appetite. I had a taste for pizza, and suggested we get a meat lover's pizza. Everybody was so hungry there was no way an objection was about to be raised. Albert and Hope waited in the car, while Joe and I went inside to place the order.

As soon as we walked inside I recognized Lisa Cooper siting in the waiting area. She had already ordered her pizza, and was so engrossed in a newspaper, she never looked up.

Lisa was the starting center on the girls' basketball team, our senior year in high school. She was six feet five inches tall, with a curvy full figure. She wore her dark brown hair straight and about shoulder's length. She was a redbone, with quite attractive features. It was her sister Gail Cooper, who I was seriously fond of, and whom seeing her reminded me of.

One hot day, a couple of years back, I had pulled off an armed robbery in Newport, and was laying low in Tri City as a precautionary measure. The streets at home were hot, and the Newport's police department's armed robbery division was hot on our trail. While there, I did some shopping to pass the day. I was walking out of one of the downtown stores, when I saw a girl from a distance walking into a women's boutique. She wore a blue halter top, and some white, hot pants. The shorts were a popular fashion during that time, and lots of women loved to wear them. She also had the most amazing pair of legs and body I had ever seen! Up until that point in my life, I had always thought there wasn't a pair of legs or body that could compare with my home girl Kari, and her Aunt Bertha, but here it was. Right before my very eyes.

I tried my best to walk away without engaging the image already seared in my mind, but I couldn't. I was as attracted to her as a moth is to a flame. I couldn't leave without seeing the face attached to such a perfectly chiseled body. I tried to catch her by yelling out to her to get her attention, as I walked as briskly as possible towards her.

"Excuse me ma'am, my I have a moment of your time?" When she turned around to face me, I was totally shocked to discover it was Gail Cooper. She had changed since I'd last seen the pretty little girl. She had blossomed into one of the most gorgeous women I'd ever laid my eyes on.

She wore her hair in a medium size curly afro, and a smile so brilliant it seemed to set off all my senses. Her breast stood at attention, and the print of her nipples enhanced the sensuality of the garment attempting to conceal them.

I began to sweat profusely, and my heart was pounding so loudly within my chest, it seemed to be the only sound that was recognizable to me. I tried to speak, but my voice failed me, and only a squeaky sound escape my throat.

"I can't believe this!" she said while laughing hysterically. Tone so intrigued with me, he's literally speechless!" She threw her head back and laughed even harder. "I would've done just about anything to get your attention when we were in high school. Here you are today in front of me speechless, and drooling.

All I could do was smile. I had to clear my throat to find my voice. "Gail, you are gorgeous!" I managed to say. "I know you have a man." I asked in the form of a statement instead of a question.

"No, I don't." she replied. "Why? Are you interested in being my man?" I couldn't believe what I was hearing. I was trying to figure out if she were joking. She had spoken the words I'd dared not to dream of hearing. I became putty in her hands from that point on. I didn't quite know how to handle the sudden rush of emotions. I was wondering what I could say to find out If she was serious without looking like a fool process.

I decided the best way to find out was to ask, so I did. "Are you serious? I would love to take advantage of an opportunity to get to know that side of you. I don't know you in that way at all, but I sure would like to." She smiled and slid into my arms and hugged me so tightly I could feel her pelvic pressing against me. I became intoxicated by the smell of her perfume and began to warm up. My ability to reason had been compromised by the moment, and the potential promises of ecstasy.

There was so much chemistry between the both of us, our eyes began to sparkle, and our skin glowed. The moment was so magical for the both of us, we became overwhelmed, and our lips were drawn to one another. We kissed. When our tongues met, I could taste her natural sweetness. It was as sweet as if she had candy in her mouth, but it was a flavor unlike any I had tasted.

We were so lost in each other and the kiss, we forgot we were on a busy downtown street. It was as though we were the only two in the whole wide world to me. People began to cheer, and cars honked their horns, but we were beyond the point of being interrupted. We continued to kiss until we had our fill. We eventually ended the kiss, and locked eyes as we stared at one another in amazement. Neither one of us could understand what was happening.

"When can we get together?" I asked. She explained that it was because of a previously planned engagement she would be unable to make any plans for the entire weekend. She had a beautiful voice. She was the lead singer in her home church's choir. They were headed to Kalamazoo that very night and weren't returning until late Sunday. I could stay no longer than Sunday and since there was no chance for us to get together, we exchanged phone numbers and made a promise to each other to get together as soon as possible. I promised her I was going to return to Tri City within a couple of weeks just to spend time with her. If I was unable to get away, Gail said she would be more than willing to make the trip to Newport, if it meant I would spend the entire weekend making love to her.

When we parted, I felt like I was walking on a cloud. I wasn't back in Newport a week before I began making plans to return to Tri City. I was watching the local news on the television at my mother's house, when the sharp ringing of the telephone startled me. There was nothing different about the ring and I wasn't so engrossed with the reporter's presentation to have been startled. I was surprised to hear Joe's voice on the line.

I had shared my experience with Joe about Gail. He was surprised when I told him about the church girl kissing me right out in the open downtown. While talking to him on the phone I sensed a halting in his voice, which alerted me of something being wrong. Whatever it was, I could tell he dreaded telling me. "What's wrong?" I demanded. I had enough of all the small talk.

"There's no easy way to tell you this cuz, so I'm just gonna come right out with it and tell you. Gail is dead." I was once again caught speechless, but this time I was in a state of shock. He continued by giving me the explanation for Gail's untimely death. As it turned out, Gail was smoking weed for the very first time in her life. It triggered an asthma attack, and she was unable to recover and regain her breathing. Because she was struggling to breathe, it brought about her untimely demise.

I hung up the phone devastated! I went to the living room and laid across the sofa. I began weeping. I wondered if I were being punished. I thought of all the murders I believed I'd been forced to commit. Why wouldn't death visit me through my heart, by taking from within it? The lives I had taken must have caused someone's heart to be broken, and what you put out into the universe, you get back. The people we love and care for the most, are kept within our hearts. Long after they've been buried, we still have a relationship with them. When death visits that circle, you can't help but feel the devastation. You learn a whole new respect for life and the taking of it. You will pay. Even though you may believe you've gotten away, there's a higher order of justice.

I didn't eat for a couple of days. I believed I would never find the love I wanted, simply because I had to make compromises to survive on these mean ass number streets. Sometimes it meant taking a life, and what goes around comes around. I had slipped into a deep depression.

The only person who was able to snap me out of the

depression and bring me back to my senses was Marty. She came to me, and lovingly kissed all my tears away. She listened to me attentively as I told her everything about Gail. Afterwards she expressed how fortunate I was to have shared such a touching moment with her, just before she parted from this world. "There's no way of predicting what would have been in store for the two of you. The only thing I can tell you with certainty is you must go on. Just like it says in the song, Only the Strong Survives, "There's a whole lot of girls looking for a good man like you, but you'll never meet them if you give up now, and say your life is through." She turned out to be all I needed to snap out of that depression.

When Lisa finally noticed me, a huge smile came across her face. "Tone!" she yelled as she ran across the floor towards me. I met her half way, and we hugged each other as she began to cry. Hope and Albert looked back and forth between Lisa and me and each other with puzzled looks on their faces. I saw Joe taking his time to explain something to them, after he'd ordered the pizza. I somehow knew he was explaining the situation to them. This was the very first time Lisa and I had seen each other since Gail's death.

"How have you been?" she asked as I wiped the tears from her eyes. I thought for a moment before answering her. I told her things had been going well, and I wasn't lying. Things really had been going well. I asked her how she had been. Just as I had given it some thought before answering, she also paused before answering. "I'm doing fine too. What are you doing in Tri City?"

I wasn't about to tell her I came to Tri City with the intentions of selling drugs. I merely told her I was there on business, and I'd be there for a couple of days. She pulled a pen and a piece of paper from her purse. Then she scribbled her name and number on it, before passing it to me. She insisted I called to talk to her mother before I left town. "I'm know she'd love to meet you. Gail told momma all about you and her before she passed." I promised I would call, and headed to the table to join Albert, Hope and Joe. Lisa followed me, so I introduced her. Her number was called, indicating her pizza order was ready. We said our good-byes and hugged one last time before she left to pay for her order. She looked over her shoulders, one last time, and waved to us as she walked out the door. I could tell she was still thinking of Gail. So was I.

We were enjoying a hypothetical conversation about the whereabouts of the missing remains of Jimmy Hoffa and the pizza, when we were interrupted by a sharp knock at the door. The knock was so loud, I thought they were about to announce their identity as being some form of law enforcement.

I made eye contact with Hope, then I diverted my eyes to the door, and back to her. She knew I was telling her to answer the door without using the words. She pointed to herself for confirmation she understood the meaning of the gesture. I bobbed my head up and down, so she got up and walked over to the door. "Who is it?" she asked.

A woman's soft voice answered. "I'm Robert's wife. He sent me here." I instructed Hope to let her in. Once she had entered the room, she spoke directly to Joe. "I need to speak with Tone." She announced. I got up and walked over to her. I held out my hand and informed her I was the person she sought.

I was thinking to myself, uh oh, here comes the bullshit. I was hoping there would be no problems, but I had a feeling troubled had just walked through my door. She broke my train of thought when she spoke. "Robert was arrested for an old traffic warrant. He has a probation hold on him, so we can't get him out on bond, and he doesn't go to court for few more days."

She opened her purse and pulled out a roll of bills. She handed them to me and said, "That's the one hundred dollars he owes you. He had put it to the side just in case something like this happened. He also told me to tell you, he should be out by the time you get back." I thanked her and walked her to the door. I opened the door, but before walking out the door she passed me a small folded up piece of paper. "That's our number. Call us in about a couple of weeks. We should have everything in order by then." Before she walked out the door she said, "Have a safe trip."

I felt relieved Robert had made provisions to make sure I got the money, but it was still bad news. I trusted Robert. We shared a history, plus he was hungrier than I'd ever seen him. He was doing great! At the pace he was going, we would have been finished in a couple of days. Now I had to depend upon Pee Wee.

After we had finished eating the pizza, I suggested to Joe that we catch up with Pee Wee to check on him. Joe insisted Pee Wee would be too frightened to try anything, but I knew better. I had learned not too long ago, that addiction was stronger than fear. We all got in the car and headed back to the store.

Pee Wee was standing in front of the store when we arrived. "Damn man, where you been?" he asked. "I was through about twenty minutes after ya'll left. We done missed all kinds of business. The word is out that we have the strongest shit in town. All my people tried to wait, but you know how that shit flies when you about to be sick or you're already sick. They all ended up going down the street to Tommy's." Then he reached in his pocket, pulled out a stack of folded bills and handed it to me. It appeared to be a lot of money, but it was mostly one-dollar bills.

He continued, "I even ended up selling mine!" and then he proceeded to count out twenty dollars right before my eyes. "I hope you brought something with you. I need some myself." he added. When I explained I hadn't brought anything with me, because I wasn't sure he needed anything yet, he exploded. "Aw naw man, you tripping and slipping! I need some more shit, and I need it right now. That is if you want to make this muthafucken money!" I told him I'd be right back, and once again we headed to the room.

I had made three hundred dollars and had plenty of product left. Uncle Fly requested I send money home to him daily through Western Union, but I considered it a ridiculous notion on his part to think I would continue to blindly cooperate. It seemed he had a hidden agenda, and I decided I was through cooperating with him until he came clean, and put all the cards on the table, face up.

I was ready to go home, and my impatience lead me to make a hasty decision. Pee Wee had sold the ten bags so fast, I decided to make thirty-six, so I wouldn't have to go back and forth to the room so often. Doing so was bound to raise suspicion.

When we got back to the store I gave Pee Wee twenty-four packs all at once. I sat in the car for a while watching as the people slowly came to do business with him. The flow was slow but consistent, so I decided it was the perfect time to get dinner.

Chapter Fifteen

We went to Bill Knaps to eat dinner. During my football, track, and basketball playing days, it was my favorite place to go to eat whenever we had an away from home game or meet. After I placed my order, everyone decided they wanted the same thing I had ordered. I was into eating beef back then, and their roast beef with gravy was my favorite on their menu. I had mashed potatoes, corn on the cob, and broccoli for sides, but first I enjoyed the house's chef salad with blue cheese dressing and dinner rolls.

We enjoyed the succulent three course meal, which was topped with apple pie a la mode for dessert. I finally felt as though I had an opportunity to relax and enjoy the company of Hope and my brother. We laughed and talked about how different Tri City was from Newport. Even their addicts were different. The addicts here didn't seem as bad off, nor did they seem as desperate for narcotics.

I had satisfied so many of my desires on so many levels, I was suddenly overcome with lust. It happens whenever I look at Hope after enjoying a full, satisfying meal. I guess that old saying is true. The way to a man's heart, is through his stomach. It would certainly get me in the mood to make love, but time is the only determining factor to determine if she ultimately gets in my heart or not. I wanted to make love to Hope, but there was just too much business needing of my undivided attention. I had to get back and check on Pee Wee. He was an addict, and although he had shown signs he could be trusted, I didn't trust him.

When we made it back, he was nowhere around, and we weren't the only people there looking for him. I still had twelve bags on me, so I served the waiting customers. Most of them recognized me, and respectfully greeted me in kind, before taking care of the business at hand.

We checked the projects, and talked to a few people he knew there, but no one had seen him in over an hour. We rode around and checked all his known hangout spots with no success. I got a real strange vibe, and that's when I noticed the concerned looks on Hope and Albert's faces. I had unintentionally brought the stress of the business on them both.

I explained to them the worst that could happen would be I would have to pay for whatever I'm short. I reminded them of the fact I had plenty of money at home, and I was only there to offer an opportunity to some friends of mine with a desire to reside among the wealthy. It was merely an expansion expedition. A successful one at that, I might add. It's going to be nice to have a broader base to begin building the foundation for the business upon. Tri City had the potential to fulfill that bill for us.

"I came here to see if there was a market for our product, and I have the answer to that question. I'm just trying to get as much money as I can out of the ounce I have. That's all. It's no big deal if I don't. I just want it. You can never have too much money. We don't want to hit the road dirty again. Even if it means having a clearance sell, we're not taking any unsold product home with us.!"

I was just about to give up the search, when a gut check made me want to ride by the store one last time. As soon as we arrived you could see Pee Wee nodding and scratching the side of his face. There was a cigarette hanging on his lower lip, as though it were being held in place by glue. As soon as he noticed me, he did exactly the opposite of what someone trying to run off would do. He began waving his arms wildly and calling out to me, as he walked in my direction.

He leaned his upper torso into the open car window and counted out one hundred dollars, and thirteen packs. "Where have you been?" I asked. "I've been looking for you." Which just so happens to have been my second mistake.

My first mistake was trusting an addict out of my eyesight. As long as an addict sees you, it seems to help keep them from forming idiotic dreams of running off into the sunset with everything you've left unattended. I've learned an addict cannot be deterred by fear. It is normal for an addict to face a possible self-inflected death by overdose daily. If you truly believe you can frighten a hardcore drug addict into not messing with anything he or she wants that's left unattended, then you are a fool. Some addict welcome death as a form of relief, so most threats of death often go unheeded.

The second mistake I made was letting him know I was looking for him, and I was unable to locate him. Even if he had no plans of running off, I had just unintentionally planted the seed of thought in his mind.

I let him keep the thirteen packs and instructed him to meet me in front of the store early in the morning. He wanted to know if we were on the same page as far as what

I considered early. I told him ten o'clock would be fine. He agreed to meet me at that time, and we parted ways. I had already trusted him with twice the amount he had, so I felt very comfortable in doing so once again.

I got another room for Albert, and Joe hung out with us for a little while, just reminiscing, listening to jazz and smoking Columbian gold. The events of the day had pretty much worn us all out, so this quiet time gave sleep an opportunity to catch up with us, and it did. Joe said his goodbyes, and we made plans to meet up around seven thirty in the morning. I couldn't wait to get Hope alone for obvious reasons.

I woke up before Hope. She looked so peaceful I couldn't bring myself to disturb her sleep. I laid beside her and stared at her face. Her forehead displayed baby hair which framed her face from her forehead to her temples. Her eyebrows were thick, and naturally arched. I leaned forward to get a whiff of her breath. I honestly can't think of anything that could compare with the sweet smell of her breath. Her breathing was deep and even. Her chest rose and fell as she took each breath.

She stirred, opened her eyes, and began to return my stare with a stare of her own. "Don't worry baby, I know it seems hard right now, but you're the one who sits on the throne to this kingdom. If only you could get a glimpse of yourself through my eyes, or believe in yourself as I do, I believe you would understand. If only that were possible."

She ran her fingers along the side of my face and flashed her beautiful smile. "You hungry?" she asked. I nodded yes in reply, but I was thinking of how hungry I was for her love making. She read my mind, laughed and reminded me it was me who fell asleep and left her hanging. We hadn't made love for that very reason for what seemed like an eternity. "You still tired?" she asked.

I wanted to take her like a stallion takes a mare. She began submitting to my whims and allowed me to have my way. "Let's do it so we can eat." she whispered in my ear. "I always have a huge appetite after we fuck!" she purred before giggling.

I looked around the room and realized most of the things in the room were antique. There had been no renovations done at this establishment, so everything was as it was in the nineteen twenties. There was a large mirror standing on a stand in the corner. I positioned the mirror, so we could see ourselves, and mounted her doggy style. It was the first time I had ever been able to please my viewing senses in such a way. We looked amazing to me. Eventually our eyes locked, and heaven was just a few strokes away.

We had already showered and gotten dressed, when Albert knocked on the door. "Ya'll up?" he asked. I answered simply by opening the door. When he walked in it was obvious from the way he smelled, and the way he was dressed, he was ready to get out. "Man, I'm hungry!" he stated as he looked around the room. I was wondering what he was looking for when he asked, "Do they have maid service in this old ass joint?"

After laughing I answered, "We'll find out soon enough, but for now let's go to the International House of Pancakes and get something to eat." Hope let me know she thought it was a great idea and headed out the door. Albert and I were in hot pursuit.

After enjoying our breakfast, we headed to the store to check on Pee Wee. My heart nearly stopped when I saw all the activity around the store, but no sign of Pee Wee. I cussed myself for trusting him. I knew better. I sat there thinking, maybe Joe would know where to find him. I didn't want Albert or Hope to sense I thought or felt anything might be wrong. I struggled with my demeanor as I tried my best to appear as confident and clam as possible, but on the inside, I was experiencing pure rage.

After catching up with Joe, we drove to several of the places he frequented. There was no sign of him anywhere. Mid-evil thoughts began to form in my mind once I realized he was hiding from me. I had no idea what I would do once I caught up with him, so I no longer wanted Hope or my brother around. There was a possibility I would be unable to contain the savage within me. Whenever possible I never commit certain acts in front of witnesses. There is no statute of limitation on some offenses, and I don't believe in leaving any witnesses behind in those type of situations. Life takes uncontrollable twist and turns, and with the passing of time fate can often change one's perception, but as far as of right now, I will never intentionally put a loved one in a position whereas I would have to make such a difficult decision.

Once I made eye contact with Joe, I winked and said, "I bet that muthafucka is still knocked out." I laughed and told Albert, "I need you to take Hope home. This is going to take longer than I expected." Hope looked at me with a concerned look on her face and demanded to know the truth about what was going on. She studied my facial expression, and my body langue for any clues of hidden clues.

I smiled and went straight Hollywood on her ass. I assured her everything was fine. With Robert in jail, and Pee Wee appearing to be shiftless and lazy, I was going to have to sell my product myself, and there was no way to tell how long it was going to take. She listened to my explanation and gave me her smile of acceptance. We headed to Joe's house to get his mother's car.

It didn't take long before Albert and Hope were packed and was on the road. I promised Hope I'd be home in a couple of days, and she promised me she'd be at the house waiting for me. I watched as they pulled away from the curb, and realized it was only our second time being apart since we started hanging out together.

Once they were out of our sight, I dropped the pretense and alerted Joe to my true gut feelings. My gut feelings, along with the collaboration of all the facts, led me to conclude Pee Wee had run off. "He ain't that crazy!" Joe insisted. I knew he had not only ran off, but he was also trying to lay low hoping I would have to leave town. My gut has never wrong.

As we walked to the car, I explained what I believed was going on. "He knows he doesn't have to hide for too long. I don't live here, and sooner or later I'll have to move on. He's gambling on me not being able to stay here for too much longer, and he'd be right!"

I stopped talking and looked around, as Joe unlocked the car doors. After we climbed in the car I continued, "I'm leaving in a couple of days. I can't sell what I have left, and hunt for his ass at the same time. He's knows this, so I must get busy with the task at hand. It's a good thing good dope sells itself."

I posted up in front of the store, and caught all the customers myself, while Joe rode around searching for Pee Wee. I had a great day. I nearly sold everything I had on a breakdown scale, but Joe's day didn't go so well. Pee

Wee was nowhere to be found, just as I had suspected. I felt horrible, because I had made the wrong call. It only cost me one hundred dollars, but it shouldn't have happened. I was impatient, and it was during that moment of weakness that I went against everything I knew about junkies.

The room was paid up for another day, so I told Joe to drop me off there. I needed to be alone. I had made too many mistakes lately. It was a must that I do a little reassessing and reflecting. As I was getting out of the car Joe called out to me. He asked if he could have a little bit of the heroin for himself to use. I was shocked! I had no idea he used the drug.

"You get high?" I asked. I can tell he was caught off guard by not only my question, but my tone of voice. I had shared my struggles with heroin with him, and I was seriously disappointed to discover his lack of respect for the horrible lifestyle it could lead to. I don't judge, and it was his life to lead. I was going to give him fifty dollars for all the running he had done for me that day, but he asked before I could give it to him. I went up to the room alone and prepared a sixty, dollar bundle for him. He had a large smile on his face when I handed it to him. He was completely satisfied.

While sitting alone in the room, beating myself up, it occurred to me I hadn't called Hope to make sure she made it home safely. She should have arrived earlier that day. When I called I was surprised when Uncle Fly answered the phone. I had called collect, and he answered. I was a little surprised by his tone of voice. He sounded very agitated. "Why haven't you called me?" he asked. I told him I hadn't thought of calling him. I also apologized for the oversight. "Well how's it going?" he asked. It sounded as though he was angry, so I omitted the part about the situation with Pee Wee.

"I still have plenty left. I was unable to please the people I wanted to land. They weren't too thrilled by the product. They are getting some shit out of Chicago that is so good. What we have just can't compete with it." I reported. Before he was able to respond, I added, "I also have eight hundred dollars in cash. I would've had more, but I gave my brother gas money."

He interrupted, "And that's why I thought you had pulled some bullshit." He said in a voice that wasn't so harsh. "I wondered why you would send them back and stay up there yourself alone with no ride home." I explain to him how the people didn't want what I had, so I had to get in the mud and grind the sack off. Simply put, I had to sell it myself without the advantages of a house for a location. It's a lot easier for me to get around and handle my business, when I'm alone. That is the reason I sent them back. "I understand that." he said in a voice that was finally calm.

"Where's Hope?" I asked. He told me she had been there earlier but said she would wait for me over her aunt's house. I told him I'd call him when I was on my way home and hung up. That was a red flag for me. Hope and I had already discussed what we were going to do. She knew I didn't have her aunt's phone number. She never would have changed our plans unless something wasn't right at home.

I called my brother, and he told me he had dropped Hope off hours ago on Pacific. She promised to call him whenever she heard from me, and that's the last time he had seen or heard from her. Things didn't add up. If she was already there waiting on me, why would she leave? I had too much going on, and I still hadn't given up on the possibility of finding Pee Wee. I had to get back to Newport but what concerned me the most was the fact that there was no way I would be able to sell everything I had left. I was going to have to transport the drugs back to Newport on the bus.

I called Gail's mother out of respect, and to see how she was doing. She answered the phone, and when I informed her it was me, she seemed very pleased. We talked for quite a while before she asked me where I was staying. I told her I was staying at a hotel.

"Oh no! You'll have to stay with us and allow me to cook you a home cooked meal. I know you haven't had one since you're staying in a hotel." I begged her to give me a rain check. I told her I had plans to stay a lot longer, but something came up at home that needed my immediate attention. She hesitated before asking. "I need a huge favor. I have a diamond cluster ladies ring. It's been appraised at ten thousand dollars. This is a small town, and all the pawn shops are owned by one family. By working in cahoots, they're trying to force me to accept their offer to take it in pawn for nine hundred dollars. If I sold the ring, I still would only want two thousand dollars for it. Could you give me two thousand for it?"

"I'm sorry mam, but I don't carry that kind of money." Then she asked me was it at all possible for me to take the ring with me to Newport and send her the two thousand dollars owed her, after I had sold it. I saw nothing wrong with doing it for her. Since she was Gail's mother, I saw it as opportunity to do something in a roundabout way for Gail. I told her I didn't have a car, and she would have to bring the ring to me. She told me since she wasn't feeling like getting out right then, she was going to send Lisa with it. That was fine with me. I promised her I'd wait on Lisa before I turned in and said my goodbyes.

A little while later I heard a light knock at my door. I opened the door and let her in. She had a beautiful smile, but she noticed I was about to smoke some weed, and her facial expression changed. I felt horrible. It wasn't my intentions to remind her of Gail's demise, and it appeared to be exactly what I had done. I immediately began apologizing. "Oh no! I'm so sorry. I just wasn't thinking. I didn't mean to remind you of anything painful."

She quickly corrected me, "No Tone, you're cool. I smoke myself." What a relief it was. I lit up the joint and after hitting it a couple of times, I passed it to her. I think it was a combination of things, but it seemed the higher I got the sexier she looked to me. I found myself wanting to touch her, but out of respect, I diverted my gaze away from her long shapely legs. This woman stood six, foot five inches tall, so when she sat down and stretched out, it seemed like her legs went on forever! I kept my thoughts to myself.

I noticed Lisa was openly staring at my crotch. She eventually commented. "Either you have a huge dick, or it's hard." She blushed and added, "I can't believe I said that out loud. I must be high." Then she began laughing and coughing, while attempting to pass me the joint. The truth of the matter was I did have an erection, and even though I thought it wasn't visible, I obviously was wrong.

"Have you and my sister ever fucked?" Lisa boldly asked. I was caught completely off guard by the question, so my immediate response was to ask, why. She stated "If ya'll have fucked we can't do nothing, but if ya'll haven't I'd love to do something right now. I haven't had a man in months, and right now I'm horny as hell!"

I wanted to jump to my feet and tell the truth. "Hell naw!"

and start taking off my clothes. The idea of having sexual intercourse with her was driving me crazy. I had never had sex with someone taller and bigger than myself. Instead, I told her Gail and I had done it several times, and I watched as her shoulders slumped, and it was obvious disappointment had overtaken her.

I couldn't believe I had not only blocked a sexual encounter with Lisa Cooper, but I ruined the possibilities of there ever being any future encounters with her. As badly as I wanted Lisa, it was too grey of an area for me to feel comfortable. Even though in reality Gail and I had never consummated our relationship, it didn't feel quite right to me to have intercourse with her sister, so I lied.

"I feel so awkward now. How embarrassing." She said as she lowered her head. I begged her not to feel any kind of way about it. I pointed out the undeniable fact that I wanted her just as badly. Men can fake a lot of things, but we can't fake an erection, and I was still quite erect. I tried to make her understand. I had never been with a woman as tall, sexy, and beautiful as her. She laughed and add, "I guess you have a point. I was excited because I had never been with a man as tall and handsome as you, or with a dick that big."

We both were laughing as she began fumbling through her purse. When she removed her hand from her purse, the entire room lit up with brilliant colors and lights. It was the ring! I hadn't expected it to be as beautiful as it was, but for ten thousand dollars, I should have. It was a very impressive piece. It was a diamond ring made with a cluster of thirteen diamonds. Each diamond appeared to be about a half of a carrot in size.

"Here it is." She stated as she handed it to me. A low

whistle escaped my lips as I handled the magnificent piece. "I guess you and my mom have worked everything out." I had the perfect person in mind to fence it too. I was thinking about Godfather, a fence out of Anderson Alabama who had moved to Newport. His natural name was Freddie Anderson, but he was better known as the Godfather. He was a huge man. He stood about six foot, three inches tall, and weighed well over three hundred pounds. He always was puffing or chewing on the end of a fat stogie. He always sported a popular Borsalino hat. Borsalino was the trademark name, but the style of hat was better known in the black community as a godfather hat. The ladies were absolutely crazy about him.

Godfather started out with a trucking company in Alabama, and then he moved to a suburb of Newport. Not too much longer after he was settled, he established a waterbed factory. After his businesses became extremely successful and lucrative, he invested his fortune in several different business ventures, and became a millionaire. After becoming a millionaire, he got into the drug business, and became a fence. He and I were extremely close. I knew if the ring was truly worth ten thousand dollars, Godfather would gladly give me five thousand for it.

I decided at that moment I had to get back to Newport, as soon as possible. This was absolutely my last night in Tri City. I just could not shake the feeling that something horribly was wrong at home. Hope was my world, so I didn't care that it meant Pee Wee would get away owing me one hundred dollars. I no longer cared that I was going to get on the Greyhound bus with about a quarter of a once, of heroin.

I wrote down my mother's phone number and handed it to Lisa. I instructed her to make sure her mother got the number. We hugged and said our goodbyes. After she had left, I called the Greyhound bus station to get the scheduled times the buses were leaving out, headed for Newport. I planned to catch the first thing smoking out of there in the morning.

Chapter Sixteen

I arrived in Newport after an uneventful departure, and it was still quite early. My brother picked me up at the station, and I gave him directions to Hope's aunt's house. It was only a few blocks from Pacific. Albert used the time during the ride to inform me of all he had done to get enrolled in school. All he had left to do was register for classes. I began to get excited about the thought of returning to campus life. It had been a while since I had attended school. Going back to school this time would be extra special, because I would be doing it with my younger brother.

Hope was so happy to see me, she gave me a huge hug. She held me so tightly and so long, I sensed something was wrong. "What's wrong baby?" I asked. She merely lowered head and stared at the ground before telling me we had to talk. She looked at my brother and back at me indicating she didn't want to speak in front of him. I understood she was asking if we could wait until we were alone. I searched her eyes for any clues of what to expect, and what I saw horrified me. She was nothing but a shell of the woman I had last seen. There was no longer a sparkle in her eyes. The glow of her skin, and her aura, was no longer prevalent. The shadow of gloom had already cast its' shadow, engulfing her and it snuffed out her soulful light.

Once we were in the car, I asked Albert to run us to Pacific. Before Albert could turn the key in the ignition, Hope interrupted with a resounding, "No! Can we please just go to your mom's house, so we can talk?"

Now I knew. Whatever it was that was bothering her, had something to do with Uncle Fly. "Okay baby if that's what you want." I said in response to her request. "Take us to Momma's house." I was trying to hide my dread, but I felt I was about to have my world rocked. Whatever it was Hope had to tell me, was going to alter the course of my life, and I knew it.

Albert hung out upstairs with us long enough to smoke a joint. Hope was distant and aloft, so Albert got the hint. Hope desperately wanted to be alone with me. I kind of welcomed the delay of the dreaded news Hope had to share. I was unintentionally stalling. Eventually Albert said his goodbyes. I thanked him and gave him some money for his trouble and gas before he departed.

Hope stared in my eyes as though she were trying to find words to speak, but they were stuck in her throat. Her eyes began to water, but she was still unable to speak. A rage was beginning to well-up within me, and I realized I had to calm myself. It wasn't going to make things any easier for Hope if I displayed uncontrollable fury before she was even able to speak.

I broke the ice as well as the silence by telling her about Pee Wee. "I was right about my thoughts. Pee Wee was missing in action." I began. I told her the whole truth about my concerns about her and Albert. I didn't like seeing signs of them stressing. So, I concealed my anxiousness, and sent them home. I told her all about the ring, and how much money we stood to make off the deal.

"Let me see that ring!" she demanded jokingly. Her demeanor had changed. I had succeeded in lightening up her mood, even if it were only for a moment. "Damn! This is the coldest ring I've ever seen in my life! Are all these real diamonds?" she asked. I assured her they were. She held the ring up to allow the lights to hit it. She was admiring it when she suddenly asked, "Can I wear it until you sell it?" I thought about it for a moment before deciding it was an excellent idea. This way she could enjoy wearing it. It had to be kept in a safe place until I was ready to sell it. What safer place could there be, other than on her finger.

There had been enough stalling between the both of us. It was time to deal with our issues. I wanted to know what had happened, even though I felt I didn't want to hear what happened out loud. "Now tell me what's wrong?" I finally asked.

She looked at the floor as she began to speak. She said she went straight to Pacific just as we had planned. She was still tired when she arrived, so she decided to lay across the bed to take a little cat nap. While she was asleep, she was suddenly awakened by the sound of Uncle Fly's and Big Foot's voices. They were talking, and she overheard Uncle Fly mention me. He was telling Big Foot how much he would hate to fuck me up, but if I had fucked up his money, he would. She said that is when Big Foot interrupted and told Uncle Fly he always picks the wrong young niggas to work with him. He even suggested Uncle Fly should give one of his nephews a chance. She said she made the mistake of thinking it was her cue to clear up the misunderstanding. She believed they needed to know the truth about everything being alright.

She stepped in the room, and politely asked to be

excused, as she interrupted their conversation. She said their startled faces was a good indicator they thought they were alone. Before she was able to say a word, Uncle Fly snapped, "Where the fuck is Tone?" He asked in an aggressive, angry, nasty tone.

"I tried to tell him you were still in Tri City and you'd be back as soon as you were finished, but before I could finish the sentence, he called me a bitch and told me to, "Shut the fuck up!" That's when I noticed he was drunk, and I never saw him angry before.

She shook her head as though the memory made her shudder, then she continued. "He told me don't nobody wanna hear that shit, and he was slurring. His tone of voice made me nervous, so I decided it would be best if I left the house. I was heading for the door, when Uncle Fly ordered me to return to the bedroom, until he and Big Foot finished talking.

"After waiting for a while, Big Foot came in the room, and ordered me to take off my clothes. Of course, I refused and begged Big Foot not to hurt me, but he snatched me off the bed, and began tearing my clothes off. I screamed as loud as I could for him to stop, and for Uncle Fly to help, but I could hear his laughter from the next room.

"He threw me across the bed and slapped me across my face. He told me to take off my panties, or he would. I tried to get him off me, but he was just too big and strong. He slapped me across my face again and told me to stop fighting, but I didn't. I was scared to death. I screamed your name when I knew I wasn't going to be able to stop him. I fought with all my might, but he ripped my panties off and raped me."

"When he finished, he laughed, and told me they knew

you had fucked up and they were going to fuck you up whenever you got back. They sat in the living room laughing, drinking and talking for about an hour, before they eventually left. I overheard them talking about going to get some more to drink. I took my first opportunity to escape. I gathered a few of my things and left you a note telling you I would be waiting at my aunt's house and left."

That explained how Uncle Fly knew about Hope's aunt. I was furious. I felt a hot tightness in my chest, and constrained energy and rage fighting for a way out of my guts. All I wanted to do was kill, and I desired redemption for my now damaged relationship. I had never been that angry before in my life! I made a declaration in my heart for Uncle Fly and Big Foot to be my enemies for life. I would seek revenge at all cost.

Hope studied my face before speaking and asked me, "What are you going to do?" I didn't immediately answer, because I had no idea where the pain would lead me. "What are you thinking? You're scaring me." She managed to say as I rose to my feet. I retrieved my pistol from my suitcase and put it comfortably in the waistband of my pants

There wasn't a staircase to reach the attic, so you had to literally climb the wall to reach it. I climbed up to the attic and pulled my sawed-off double-barreled shotgun from under a comforter I had it hidden under, along with a box of shells. I attached the butt of the shotgun to a special shoulder harness I had made. The harness made it a lot easier to carry and conceal. I pulled my jacket on over the shotgun, and against Hope's pleads and protest, I gently kissed the side of her face. I seared as much of her beauty as I could to my consciousness, because it was very possible it could be my last time ever seeing her. I left without another word or thought.

Pacific was my destination, and killing Uncle Fly, Big Foot or anyone else who tried to stop me on my way in or out, was my sole mission.

As I walked the two-mile distance to Pacific, I tried to come up with a plan. I could very easily creep up the back stairs undetected, and the back door was so flimsy I could kick it in, with little to no effort. Therefore, the rear would be my point of entry.

If Uncle Fly's car was in the garage, it meant he was inside. If I was fortunate, I would also find Big Foot inside. I could feel my heart pounding with each step I took. I did my best to remain on the side streets and hug the shadows of the trees. I needed the shadows for assistance in my feeble attempt at concealing my weapons in broad-daylight.

In my mind I had already blasted Uncle Fly and Big foot several times with my shotgun. I hated them, and I could not wait to extract my fair share of their blood, flesh and pain. It seemed like the closer I got to my destination, the harder my heart pounded. I was still so blinded by my rage I wasn't sure if I had seen any people on my way there or not. At one point I broke out into a full sprint. I no longer cared about being cautious. I was not out of breath when I stopped running. The only reason I stopped was because I had come to my senses in time to realize my running could attract unwanted attention.

Finally, upon arriving at Pacific, I peered through a side window of the garage. I was driven to the brink of insanity to discover the garage was empty. Uncle Fly wasn't there, so Big Foot definitely wouldn't be.

I found a blind spot in the corner of the garage that would've made it difficult for a person entering the structure by vehicle to see me. I laid in wait for hours, but he never showed. I had accomplished nothing by laying there for hours. I thought of nothing, except how horrible it must have been for Hope to have this giant of a man forcing himself upon her. She needed me, and I wasn't there.

She used to brag to me about how safe being my woman made her feel. I was sure she no longer felt that way. I knew my news of nothing happening upon my return, was only going to succeed in frustrating and disappointing her more. There was nothing I could do. They weren't there. My desire to seek an opportunity to kill, would have to wait.

I went back to my mother's house. I found Hope in one of the upstairs bedrooms. She was laying across the bed asleep. I woke her and told her everything that happened, or I should say, I explained why those two were still breathing. She did her best to pretend it didn't matter, but I knew it did.

We laid down together that night, and as I held her in my arms I could sense the Hope I held in my arms was no longer the Hope I loved. This Hope was distant. This Hope was angry. This Hope had been touched by the thorns of life, and her opened wound bled until there was nothing left except a harden, bitter soul. I recognized it from experience. When this happ ens to you, there are no words that offer instant gratification. All you can do is look within yourself, and with tears falling from your eyes you beg yourself to be strong, and to hold on.

When I woke up that morning she was gone. I jumped from the bed and ran towards the stairs as I called out her name, but she was gone. I cussed aloud! I was angry at myself for being so worn out, I fell asleep. She had left unnoticed. After giving it some thought, I wondered had she got any sleep at all.

I tried unsuccessfully several times to catch Uncle Fly or Big Foot slipping. I had so much trouble finding them it became obvious they were ducking and dodging me. They hadn't known me very long, but it wasn't a secret to them how I felt about Hope. It didn't take someone with exceptional intellectual ability to figure out what was in my heart. They knew what they had done.

Through Uncle Lucky, Godfather got in touch with me. He had gotten a semitrailer full of high grade marijuana, but he only had a heroin clientele. During that same time, Uncle Fly had a lot of heroin to move, but only had a marijuana clientele. I sat down with Godfather and explained the simple solution to the dilemma. He needed Uncle Fly just as badly as Uncle Fly needed him.

They were both very smart and resourceful men. All I had to do was introduce them and get out of their way. I could have tried to get in the middle of their business, but it wasn't necessary. It was a no-lose situation for me. I wanted to repair my relationship with Uncle Fly. I'd come to the realization it was the only way I would ever get an opportunity to kill Big Foot, and I was determined to do so. His lustful desires to have Hope had destroyed my world. I had nothing to lose by taking his life.

Godfather informed me that he and Uncle Fly had struck up a deal. They were going to become partners. The most shocking part to me was their decision to put me in charge of all of Uncle Fly's heroin. I was a partner. All I had to do was teach them all I knew about the heroin trade. How to cut it, and with which ingredients. How to market it, and how much to charge. It was all mine, but it was under two conditions. I had to leave Unck out of our business. He was quite adamant about that point. He told me they understood he was my father, so they would never demand I have nothing to do with him, but he was never to be included in anything we did. "If you need to talk to your father before making the decision, we understand." He concluded.

"I will have a talk with my father, but only to inform him about my decision. I'm my own man. I've been on my own since I was twelve years old. There is no way I'm going to pass on such a great opportunity. No way. You can count me in."

I hadn't heard from Hope in days. I had absolutely no idea where to find her. Her aunt hadn't heard anything either and was becoming a bit concerned herself. It was so unlike her to not check in daily. After I put some of my fellas on the case, she was located. She had been spending a lot of time at a dope-house on 123rd and Jackson, and she was snorting a lot of heroin. I didn't want to believe the rumors, but the source was too reliable to ignore.

I hung out over my mother's house for quite a few days, hoping Hope would show up or call. My mother told me my heart was broken, and I needed to move on and forget about her. I laughed it off, as though there was no way I was down in the dumps over a girl. I told her and my Aunt Henrietta all about the ring, and how much I stood to make out of the deal. "That's why I'm so concerned." I clarified. "I haven't seen or heard from her in days, and now there's a rumor she's using drugs."

We were sitting on the front porch when my sister came to the door and told me Hope was on the phone and wanted to speak with me. I ran to answer the phone.

Hope told me she was alright, and the rumors were true about her snorting heroin. "Why?" I asked. She stated it made her numb to all the pain she was experiencing. She also informed me she had a new man. She told me they get high together. She said she really hates getting high alone, and she refused to drag me down with her.

"But I love you Hope. What about that? I thought you loved me too. Don't do this to us." I pleaded. She was quiet for a moment before speaking. Her tone of voice was harsh when she told me it was too late for us. Too much had happened, and not enough had done, was the way she put it.

I was crushed. I was trying to think of something I could say that would convince her to see me in person. I believed if I could see her face to face, I would be able to persuade her to give us another chance. Then I thought about the ring.

"What about the ring?" I asked. She admitted she had pawned the ring. I was desperately hoping she had pawned it to a reputable pawn shop, instead of some want to be dopeman. I knew it would be possible for me to convince her to bring me the pawn slip to me, if she pawned it to a shop. "Did you pawn it to a pawn shop?" I asked.

"I pawned it at Sam's pawn shop on Michigan Avenue. I have the ticket, I just don't have a way of getting to you." I suggested she tell me where she was, and I could come to her. "No, I'm not stupid Tone." she answered. "We are through. I'm not going to drag you down with me.

I changed the urgency of the conversation by asking how much she had pawned it for. Her answer was almost hilarious. She pawned it for one hundred dollars. I suggested she catch a cab to my mother's house and bring me the pawn slip. I promised to take care of the cab fare to wherever she wanted to go. To my delight, she agreed, and promised to be there shortly.

I went back to the front porch to rejoin my mom and Aunt Henrietta. "What did she say?" my aunt asked. Before I could answer her first question, she asked another "Does she still have the ring?" I told her Hope had pawned the ring for one hundred dollars. "What!" she exploded in shock and anger. "You should beat her ass whenever you see her!"

After a while Hope showed up in the cab, just as she had promised. She got out and stood next to the car. She waved for me to come to her. I thought I was paying the cab driver and sending him on his way, but Hope insisted I give her the money, so she could be on her way. I gave her a twenty-dollar bill, and she handed me the pawn slip.

When she went to get in the car something inside of me snapped. I was the typical young, confused black man, totally out of touch with his emotions. I had no idea how to express my pain, or sense of lost. All I'd ever known, seen, or understood was violence. For me, violence was the answer for everything.

I grabbed Hope by her beautiful, long pony-tail and drug her away from the car. I punched her in the chest so hard it knocked her to the pavement. I was in the middle of delivering some very carefully-placed body shots, when I suddenly heard my mother's voice calling out to me. She was pulling on my shirt while begging me to stop.

I backed off her, which allowed her the room necessary to get to her feet. She quickly ran to the cab. I was about to pursue her, but I heard Marty's voice saying, "Let her go baby." It occurred to me at that moment we were right in front of Biggum's house. Marty, her mother, her sister and her brother were all on the porch. They were all standing on their feet. I was proving once again to be the type ugliness you may encounter when dealing the ignorant confused off-springs of slaves. All my sisters were outside playing, but they stopped playing just to watch me act a fool.

I watched as Hope hopped in the cab and quickly closed the door. As the cab pulled away from the curb, and eventually out of my sight, my feet felt like they were stuck in concrete. I was so ashamed for the way I had acted, but no one dared to speak a word. I was ill for days after the incident. I truly felt there was nothing worth living for.

I was sitting on the sofa in my mother's house feeling sorry for myself and watching television, when suddenly there was a loud knock at the door. When you are raised in the black community you were taught to knock respectfully at someone's door. The only time you received a loud knock at your door was because there was an emergency, or it was the police.

"Who's that knocking at my door like they're the Police!" my mother asked while showing displeasure for the sign of disrespect. After taking a quick peek, while being careful not to be detected, I informed her I had no idea who the white men at the door were. "Let me get it!" she insisted.

Black women have learned from years of dealing with slavery, the KKK era, Jim Crow, and the so-called American just-us system, to act as a shield between the white establishment and their men folk. What my mother was doing was instinctive. It was something inherited through her DNA. "May I help you?" she asked while opening the door.

"We are United States Marshalls mam, and we need to speak with Marvin." The tallest one spoke, as he nodded his head in my direction while peering over my mother's shoulder. His partner kept his eyes pinned on me.

The words brought about thoughts of horror. I'd gotten away with committing so many crimes, I couldn't think of what they possibly could have wanted. I rose to my feet and followed their suggestion to sit at the dining room table.

They were interested in me for an uttering and publishing case. When I was younger I cashed several stolen United States Treasurer checks for six hundred dollars apiece. A friend of mine was working at the bank as a teller. She would cash any kind of check I brought to her if it was not a personal check. She had gotten caught after years of enjoying the extra income. As part of her plea agreement she turned in the names of everyone she had cashed checks for. My name was at the top of her list.

A handwriting analysis was conducted on me, while I sat there at the table. It concluded the signature was indeed done in my own handwriting. I was instructed to turn myself in at the Federal building early Monday morning. At that time, I would be booked and released on a personal recognizance bond. I was informed I would receive probation if I made it to all my appointed court dates. Afterwards they left without incident.

That bit of reality was a slap in the face for me. I didn't have a good reason at all to explain why I hadn't begun the registration process to enroll in Jochannan College at Newport. It was going to be important for the magistrate to know I wasn't an idled young black man. Jailtime would still be up to a judge's discretion at sentencing, so it's wise to be working, going to school or both.

I caught the bus up to the school to have a talk with the head basketball coach, Phillip Riley. He had once recruited me. He took my mother and my aunt to a game in hopes of landing me for his program. I caught him in his office and expressed my desire to participate in the school's basketball program. If he was excited about the prospects of having me in his program, he hid it brilliantly.

"We're having an informal practice today at Considine's Recreational Center at three o'clock this afternoon. Be there and I'll take a good look at you and decide if I want to offer you a scholarship for next season or not."

"Next season! That's too far off." I said in an urgent tone of voice. Coach Phil then explained everything to me. He had already committed all his scholarship funds for the school year. There wouldn't be an opening until next season. In return, I came clean about my legal problems. He promised me if he saw anything in my basketball game during the informal practice that he felt he needed for his program, he would find a way to get the funds for me to attend school this season.

Although I had been promised probation, I wanted some added insurance. I knew better than to waltz into a courtroom expecting probation while not being employed or attending school. I was going to need all the ammunition I could get to make probation a viable option for the magistrate.

The Considine Rec Center was in a section of the city called the North End. It had been a while since I had played, so I was hungry. When I was called upon to enter the game, I had an edge on the other participants. I was desperate. I was playing for my life, and it showed. The play I believe convinced the coach to place me on the team was when the starting center shot a skyhook over the second-string center. I jumped higher than both of them with ease and blocked the sky hook shot attempt out of play.

The entire gym erupted, as expressions of shock and

bewilderment were displayed. The play was the perfect play for a demonstration of my gifted jumping ability. The coach could hardly contain his excitement, but he was able to gather himself before anyone noticed. My talent was raw, and my potential was obvious.

"Yeah we can use you." He told me as he bobbed his head up and down. "We will work the money issues out through financial aid. Just report to the Financial-Aid office and tell them I sent you." He also told me to get enrolled and pay attention to the student bulletin board located in the Student Center for announcements concerning the basketball team tryouts but until then just enjoy the campus and classes. I felt a sense of accomplishment because it was going to be impressive to be attending a major college and a member of a nationally ranked basketball team once I was in front of the magistrate.

I went to my mother's house to get the pawn ticket. I solicited Marty's assistance for a ride to do all the necessary running around that had to be done. She drove me to the pawn shop to get the ring out of pawn. Afterwards we went to see the God Father. God Father told me he believed the ring was worth more than twelve thousand dollars and gave me six thousand dollars. He suggested we wait until we could get it appraised, but it wasn't necessary.

Mrs. Cooper had shown such unwavering confidence in my integrity and character, she hadn't called once to check to see how things were going. It was with great joy when I contacted Ms. Cooper to get the necessary information to send her the two thousand dollars she had requested. When I told her, it was done, and I was ready to send her the money, she simply said," I knew you could do it. Thank you."

Chapter Seventeen

It was time to get in touch with Fly. It was hard to imagine how dark my thoughts would become, if given the opportunity to come face to face with Big Foot. I wasn't sure I'd be able to conceal the hatred, contempt and disgust in my heart. I thought about the fact that most gangsters are force at some time or the other to deal with someone they would whether not deal with. It was the life I had chosen, and it was now the role I had to play.

I called the house on Pacific and a guy answered the phone. I didn't recognize the voice, so I asked to speak with Uncle Fly. "Oh, he ain't here. Is this Tone?" the voice asked. After letting him know it was indeed me, he told me he had been instructed to give me Uncle Fly's home number. He waited patiently while I found something to write the number down with.

When I called, Uncle Fly answered the phone. I thought I recognized his voice, so I asked, "Hey Uncle Fly is this you?" He let me know it was him, then asked me where I had been. He claimed to be asking, because he was so concerned and worried about me and my well-being. He said a lot of nice things to me. It was obvious he was extending an olive branch. Of course, I knew there was no sincerity behind any of the thoughtful things he was saying, but I didn't let on that

I knew. I told him I had been busy enrolling in school and trying out for the school's basketball team.

"That's my boy!" he yelled into the receiver of the telephone. He responded with glee, but I only found offense in his fake excitement. I knew it was all an act, so I followed his lead and pretended to be buying his act whole heartedly.

"Listen..." He continued, "I need to see you. Are you close to Pacific?" I told him I was very close, and I could walk there in about twenty minutes. He insisted it wasn't necessary and he would come to get me. I had to think of something quickly. I didn't want him to know where my mother, or Biggum lived.

"I'm on my way to the Hole to take care of something right quick. Can you pick me up there?" I asked. He inquired about how long it would take for me to get there. When I told him, I would be there in five minutes, he promised to meet me there in about twenty minutes and ended the call.

I pulled out my pistol, chambered a shell and put the safety on. I replaced it and headed out the door walking. I could've gotten Marty to drop me off, but I needed the alone time. I needed time to think. I knew at some point that evening it would be possible for me to be led into a trap, and that bit of reality made me think. By the time I reached the Hole, I knew exactly what I was going to do. I didn't care if I was being led into a trap. My mind was made up. I relished the opportunity make sure Big Foot caught a slug in the head, at the first sign of there being a setup.

As he had promised, Uncle Fly arrived. Albeit a bit late. I left the bar and went outside. I stood next to the car and took a deep breath of the night air. I looked around and noticed there was a whole new crew of youngsters hanging out on the corner like we used to do when we were that age. A few yelled out my name and waved wildly. I wave back and shouted, "What up doe?" as I climbed into the passenger's seat.

He broke the silence speaking pleasantries, but he broke the ice when he said, "You were right about the dogfood, Tone. It had been cut, but I have some real raw for you to work with now." I forced a smile and asked who cut the dope the first time. He warned me I didn't want to know. He told me he didn't want to cut it, but someone was trying to make some money on the side, by cutting my part.

I wanted to pull my pistol and splatter his brains all over the windshield, but I resisted the urge. The words he spoke nearly floored me, and I had to adjust quickly. It turned out to be life altering information for me. "It was your dad. When me and Big Foot told him, we were not going to let him do his son like that, he told us you were not his real son. He said he didn't look at you like you were really a member of his family. He said although he wished nothing but the best for you, you were nothing more than a way to get the money he needed to take care of his real family."

I was devastated. It was the last straw for me. My back was broken. Once again, I had allowed myself to be suckered into believing it wasn't me against the world. The only words I spoke out loud was when I told Uncle Fly I knew the dope game better than I knew any other game. We continued riding towards Pacific just listening to the radio without either of us uttering a single word. I caught a glance of Uncle Fly looking upon me with pity. That's when I realized the pain in my heart, was resting out in the open upon my sleeve. I had been exposed as the deeply hurt, betrayed fake son. I felt like a complete damned fool. Mercifully the ride only lasted approximately five minutes.

We went up the back stairs and entered the house through the rear. As we climbed the stairs, I thought about all the times I had hidden in the garage lying in wait for such an opportunity as this one. I didn't see Big Foot's car anywhere, so I assume he wasn't around. I dared not ask about him. It may draw suspicion since he knew what Big Foot had done to my Hope.

Once we were in the house, I noticed there were several young guys who were about my age, hanging out. They were all openly armed with large caliber pistols resting in shoulder holsters. Fly introduced me to each one-off them and told them I was his nephew. "Your things are behind the bar." he informed me. When I looked behind the bar I saw a couple of suitcases, and several large black garbage bags. He stretched out his hand and said, "Give me your keys. From now on I don't want you to come over here for anything. When you need to see me, or when you're ready to re-up you'll be coming directly to my home."

I handed him my set of keys, and he pulled out a sandwich bag full of heroin. It looked just like coffee and it had a strong vinegar smell. The sight and the smell of the drugs told me it was pure. "That's a once of raw." he added. "Just give me nine hundred dollars if you want to buy some more."

Now this was more like it. I could make some serious moves with a product like this. "How's Hope?" he asked. I knew it was a trick question to see how I would react. I caught myself and focused on the challenge before me which was being as deceitful as possible. I had to think, act, and respond quickly to appear genuine. I concealed the blood boiling affect her name passing his lips had on me.

I forced a fake sad and puzzled facial expression and responded, "I don't know? She broke up with me, and won't tell me why?" It was my turn now. I was testing him. I wanted to see how easily lying was for him and how good he was at hiding his true feelings. "She won't even talk to me." I said as I stared at the floor.

I was caught off guard again, when Big Foot slowly emerged from my old bedroom. I was surrounded by gunmen I had never seen before, but here was my opportunity to kill both Fly and Big Foot. The only problem was there were too many of them for me to make it out without being shot. The luster which had resided in my heart to sacrifice my life, if need be, just for an opportunity to kill them had tarnished. Hope and I were no longer together nor were we speaking. I would continue to seek opportunities to kill Big Foot, but I was no longer willing to sacrifice my life for an opportunity to do so.

This could've also been a setup to kill me. I had to make sure if it was, I would take Big Foot with me. It was showtime. To get as close to Big Foot as I possibly could, I flashed a broad smile from ear to ear and pretended to be delighted to see him. I went to him and gave him a huge hug, as I was saying, "I didn't know you were here!"

"I was laying across the bed getting some rest, when I thought I heard your voice. How you been doing man?" he asked with as much sincerity as he could muster. I told him I was cool, but it occurred to me that I should be trying to get out of there. I sought assistance in locating the telephone, so I could call a cab, as I looked around for the phone.

Uncle Fly quickly responded, "You don't have to do that. One of us will drop you off." I explained how I felt more secure riding in a cab with that amount of dope on me. We all knew the police very seldom stopped taxi cabs in the city, so it made sense. I called a taxi and was on my way within minutes.

Considering what I knew, I didn't want to go to Unck's house, so I took my things to my mother's house. After putting my clothes away, I measured out a couple of mack spoons of heroin and put them in a small envelope. It wasn't too late, so it was a possibility I could make a few moves or at the very least, some serious networking. I headed back to the Hole, but this time I was there solely to see Uncle Lucky.

Uncle Lucky was in the backroom with Frank Nitty when I arrived. Everybody who knew Frank called him Nitty. He was an older man and was very well known and loved throughout the city by all the major street players. His a reputation of being very knowledgeable, honorable, and a man of his word. Whenever you did business with him, it was always straight, with no bullshit. Those are very desirable qualities you can only hope to find in a individual you're trying to do business with.

I was hoping to do some business with Uncle Lucky, but before I could break the great news to him, he shared his bad news with me. He and Easy had been indicted for conspiracy to distribute a control substance, by the Feds. He had to shut down all his businesses. I was disappointed to say the least. I knew Uncle Lucky would have brought at the very least one whole ounce each day of the week.

I wasn't the only one disappointed. The news caused Nitty to express his disappointment as far as their friendship, as well as the effect it would have on his business. Uncle Lucky was his supplier. He expressed his concerns and hoped Uncle Lucky could recommend someone. I took that as my cue, and politely interrupted their conversation to let them know I too had raw for sell.

Nitty said, "If it's some good shit that can stand up to what I'm trying to do to it, I'll buy an ounce every day. I gave him the macks spoons of raw I had measured out to be tested. "Look Tone, I'm willing to pay fifteen hundred an ounce right now. He got some lactose from Uncle Lucky and pulled a mack spoon from his inside coat pocket. He then mixed two spoons of the lactose with one spoon of the raw. He took the two spoons of the mixed drugs with him to be tested.

Uncle Lucky took the remaining spoon and began snorting it. I had no objections, because I wanted to see firsthand what effect it had on snorters. Moments later, he began showing signs of the drug taking effect. He had just introduced his system to some of the strongest heroin he had ever consumed in his life. As he began scratching the side of his face, he suddenly made a dash for the restroom. He was throwing up so hard you could hear him through two closed doors. It sounded just like he was calling out to someone named Earl. When he came back, he was so high it was obvious it took all his focus and concentration to keep from nodding off. He managed to take a seat and say, "Damn!" before slowly closing his eyes.

Nitty came back a few minutes later, and excitedly stated, "Man, we're in business!" He took the last mack of raw and put some lactose on it before heading towards the door once again. "I'll be right back." He stated as he left. Uncle Lucky came out of his nod just in time, it seemed. As soon as he was fully awake he had to rush to the restroom to throw up again.

About twenty minutes later Nitty came back with a light-skinned man, with his hair in long red braids. "Tone, this is Red, my partner." We gave each other a power handshake and exchanged pleasantries. He expressed how happy he was to meet me and asked if I was sure I could get an ounce of raw like this every day. I assured him I could and promised to be capable of delivering whatever amount he desired.

"You have an ounce I can get right now?" he asked. I told him I had one close by, but it would take me about a half hour to return with it, because I was walking. Uncle Lucky threw his car keys at me, and I caught them in midair without much effort. He told me to take his car, because he wasn't going anywhere any time soon. He was already in a full nod before I could thank him. We all burst into laughter, as I walked out the door.

When I got back with the ounce, I gave Nitty what I had left. He weighed it out and it was still well over twenty-seven grams. Nitty counted out one thousand five hundred dollars and handed it to me. "I'm giving you the full amount because what you have is better than anything that has been around for years! We're all about to be rich! Your job is to keep it like this and our job is to move it. Keep it like this and you'll get a bonus every week for a job well done."

Just that quickly I was sold out and had made six hundred dollars on the fast flip. I left on foot to go see Marty. I really felt better, but thoughts of Hope soon began to tug at the strings of my heart. I loved her, missed her and I worried about her. I didn't want to be alone and Marty truly was my best friend. I wanted to share my good news with her. I knew she'd be more excited about me enrolling in school than anything else. I couldn't wait to tell her. Despite all the troubles I'd experienced, I'd just experienced a great day.

Marty was her usual unconditional loving self. Her presence was all that would have been necessary to help me reflect upon things, and her wisdom never failed me when I needed it. Her beauty, her touch, her kisses, and her loving never failed in pleasuring or comforting me. Tab was asleep with her grandmother, so I spent the night in Marty's bed for the first time. I knew it was going to blow everybody's mind to see us spending a night together in Marty's bedroom, but Marty got me up and out of there before Tab woke up. We were an undividable team, she and I.

The next morning, I called Uncle Fly, and told him I was finished. I also informed him I was ready to see him again. He told me he would be home all day, and all I would have to do was call before I came. He didn't sound the same. There was a plea in his attitude for us to squash our petty differences and get money together.

I went to check up on Albert. I was checking to make sure he had enrolled. He was of great concern to me. I didn't want my brother to become a victim of social deprivation. I felt that education was the only way to improve his employability. I didn't want him to be like me and begin embracing a culture that would lead to a life which could include incarceration or ended by death. I had already done time for murder and although I was only a juvenile it still appeared on my record as a huge blemish. I had already been denied admission to the Air Force and the Naval academies because of my record.

Albert was practicing on his bass guitar when I arrived. "What's happening." I asked. We have always been happy to see each other, but this time was special. I wanted to know if he'd completed his registration at Jochannan College at Newport. He hadn't, so I suggested we go together. I still hadn't finished. I needed to fill out my financial aid application. I knew he would also need financial aid, so we agreed that no time was better than the present to drop everything and go right then. It would give us a chance to get familiar with the campus.

We spent the entire day filling out the necessary paperwork and touring the campus. It was all official. We were now registered students, enrolled at Jochannan College. I knew the Student Center would be the place I spent most of my time as soon as I saw the setup. The music was playing, and I heard hookup conversations mingled in with academic conversations. There was food being prepared and served canteen style. The women were exactly what you would expect from a major historical black college. They were absolutely gorgeous!

It was time to get back to work, so I had Albert drop me off at the Hole. I was hoping to catch up with Nitty, and Red. Instead I ran into an old friend of mine named Ronald. He was one of the Curry brothers. He, unlike his bigtime drug slinging brother, was a heroin addict. He had been an addict for years, and never concerned himself with what others thought of him.

"What's up Dog?" he asked as he approached me. He took my right hand in his own and shook it as he hugged me with his free arm. We had always been extremely tight. His entire immediate family was quite fond of me. They lived only three blocks from my mother's house and I spent a good deal of my time there. "I don't know what's happened, but this guy she's been hanging out with is shoveling shit up her nose. He gives her all the dope she wants, and she's strung out bad now.

The information was like a kick I my gut. She had left me for another man, and he was feeding her a substance that was sure to make her dysfunctional. I hadn't talked to Hope since the day I jumped on her and beat her up, and I told him so. He told me he had heard about it, but he also heard how everybody at the spot called her new boyfriend all kinds of bitches and hoes because he didn't step to me after I beat up his woman. They all knew he would never consider checking me as an option.

Then Ronald dropped a bomb on me. "Do you want the phone number where she be hanging at? She still loves you and talks about you all the time. She tells everybody that will listen to her that she is not good for you, and she loves you too much to drag you down with her."

I knew he was telling the truth because she had uttered those exact words to me. "Okay, give me the number." I said. He wrote the number down on a piece of paper for me, slapped my hand some skin and left.

A little while later Nitty and Red showed up. "Hey little brother, you ready to do that again?" he asked. I had been sitting at the bar sipping on vodka mixed with grenadine and papaya juice while watching Kari demonstrate how she plays with a penis on a beer bottle. I was turned on and becoming sexually frustrated by the tease. Kari had always enjoyed teasing me. I had always been so attracted to her, I found myself caught in her web of sexual torture quite often.

"Yeah but I have to call first." I answered. Kari handed me the telephone from behind the bar and winked at me before walking away. I dialed Uncle Fly's number and was surprised by the unexpected sound of his voice answering the phone on the other end of the line. "Hey Uncle Fly! It's me, Tone. I'm ready to come see you."

"Okay!" he said, then he proceeded to give me instructions. "Park in the parking lot at the resturant behind the house and come into the back yard through the gate. Go to the side door and ring the doorbell. Are you coming from the Hole?" he asked. He was trying to calculate my possible time of arrival by judging the distance I had to travel. I told him I was indeed at the Hole and I would be arriving at his house in approximately twenty minutes.

I hung up the phone and handed it to Kari. I looked her directly in her eyes to make sure I had her attention and told her I'd be back. That's when she remembered and informed me of Uncle Lucky's expressed desire to see me. She said he wouldn't be there for about an hour. I assured her I would be back within a couple of hours and left with Nitty and Red.

The traffic was light, so we reached or destination at the expected time of arrival. We parked as instructed, and Red counted out fifteen hundred dollars. He handed it to me and told me to take as much time as needed. After ringing the doorbell, Uncle Fly greeted me with a huge smile.

"I was told what we have is the best in the city." he said as I was walking through the door. I informed him I had gotten the same response from everyone I used to test it. He led me to the kitchen where all his children were gathered. They were absolutely thrilled to see their newly found big cousin, and they all greeted me with a warm greetings, filled with enthusiasm. Aunt Francine came into the kitchen to give me a big hug as well.

"Were giving a party next weekend, and I expect you

to be here." she demanded. I told her I would do my best to attend, but I had started school and in order to succeed in obtaining my degree, I had to keep my priorities in order. "Awww! Order him to be here Fly, before I wind up getting in his ass!" she said as she chuckled. I laughed and promised to attend her party. I joked about not wanting to get on her bad side. "I just love college kids. They're so smart." She added before laughing, thanking me and giving me a final hug before leaving the room.

I handed him eighteen hundred dollars, and told him I needed another whole one, and the other one broken down into quarters. He instructed me to go to the basement and to wait for him. He promised to be down shortly. Thick white shag carpet covered the steps. I found the bottom step a comfortable place as any to wait.

When he came down to the basement, he lead me to a bar. He knelt behind the bar a pull up a triple beam scale. It was exactly like the ones I remembered using in the school lab. After he placed it on the bar, he placed what looked like a brick on the bar and asked me had I ever seen a kilo before. It was obvious this must have been a kilo from the expression of pride on his face, and the way it was wrapped. I had seen a kilo before, but this was different. It was my first time working out of an uncut kilo of heroin. It had a clear transparent cellophane layer on the outside, and underneath there was a layer of thin brown paper wrap, with a foreign stamp on it.

He handed me a hospital mask to put on and put one on himself. He explained to me as he was cutting a small portion of the wrapping away with a knife, "This is how it comes when it is pure and untouched." Then by using the knife, he began chopping pieces away from the brick. Even with our masks on, the smell of vinegar was extremely strong. "When you cut heroin that hasn't been cut, the mask will help to keep you from accidently becoming addicted. The mask also is to help to prevent accidental overdoses, so be very careful and wear it." he warned me. He weighed out twenty-eight grams by adding and taking away from the pieces he'd already chopped.

"There are seven grams to a quarter, fourteen for a half, and twenty-eight in a whole one. Trust me you're gonna need to get one of these" he said indicating he was referring to the scale. "Everybody is getting away from the old way of measuring everything with measuring spoons and switching to the universal metric weight system." I'd already learned the metric system in school, so it helped to place me a little ahead of the game.

"You don't have to give any breaks because what you have is pure." He then placed another brick on the bar. "This is what they call kibote. It is the garbage off heroin. It all comes from the Opium plant. First you get pure opium, and from that you get pure morphine. Heroin is the residue off morphine, and kibote is the residue off heroin." He studied my face after he had given me the information. He was checking to make sure I wasn't getting lost in his presentation.

I picked up the kibote to check it out. I checked its' consistency and it had the same smelled, taste, color and consistency as the pure heroin. "This is cut?" I asked. "You can't tell the difference between this and real dope!" I flatly stated. Uncle Fly said the only difference between the two was the kibote won't get you high. He said we get the stuff free with every shipment. It wasn't heroin, but it was the best thing you could possibly cut heroin with.

He then took a gram of kibote from its' brick and added it to a gram of heroin in a coffee bean grinder. He pressed down on its' top and the grinder came to life. The sound of the rocks being tossed about and pulverized by the machine, replaced the silence. He handed me a silver McDonald's spoon. "This is yours to keep. Take care of it. I can't get any more, and they are extremely expensive." I knew what he was saying was true. McDonald's had discontinued making the spoons, so a silver spoon had to cost at the very least one thousand dollars.

He took the drugs from the coffee grinder and placed it in a manila envelope. This is the recipe for what you've been selling. Spoon that shit up and pass out some samples. He then took my two ounces and turned it into four ounces using the kibote. He quartered one of the ounces, as I had requested, and packed each one them in a manila envelope. He packed each one of my ounces in a plastic sandwich bag. I was expecting to leave with two ounces and here I had four ounces. One for Nitty and Red and three for myself, as well as some samples.

As I was leaving, Uncle Fly stopped me and asked if I had a gun. I told him I carried a nine-millimeter, but he insisted upon seeing it. I pulled it out from the small of my back and showed it to him. He smiled with approval when he saw it. "That's a nice piece!" he said. "Make sure you take excellent care of your baby. Remember it's you and your baby against the world. Have it with you whenever you're taking care of business. It's better to be caught by the police with it, then by some rotten ass niggas in these streets without it."

Chapter Eighteen

As I was climbing back into the van, Red commented, "Damn that shit is loud as fuck! I can smell it." Nitty said it was the smell of money. Red spoke to me over his shoulder from behind the steering wheel. "We have to make a stop before heading back to the Hole. One of our spots has been out since last night, so we have to drop off some work there."

We took the freeway which led to the neighborhood and took the exit. To my amazement we pulled up in front of the place I'd been informed Hope was hanging out in. "This is your spot?" I asked. I was so excited I was unable to conceal the joy. Nitty corrected me by reminding me we were all partners. He told me it was our spot. I asked if I could go in and they both burst out laughing. Nitty asked me if I wanted to see if my ex was in there.

I was both surprised and embarrassed. I wondered how much they knew. Nitty saw my questioning expression and answered. "You are no longer under the radar little brother. You're a player in the lime light now. You're a rising young ghetto superstar. People you don't even know exist know who you are. They sit around discussing you, and your business like you were friends since childhood. Everywhere you enjoy going to spend time, will soon be considered the place to be.

"Look, the whole hood is talking about why you jumped

on Hope. She was wrong and as much as you loved her, you didn't give her a pass. You whupped her ass!"

We walked in the joint, and we were being greeted like we were celebrities. Some of the guys I had never seen in my life were greeting me and using my name to do so. I saw Hope sitting on a couch nodding. She arose once she heard our voices. Her eyes widen in surprise once she shook the cobwebs of her mind and realized it was me. She was wondering what I was doing there when Red spoke up and made the announcement. "This spot is as much your spot as it is ours. Whenever you feel the need to check things out just use your key." He handed me a key and turned to a tall dark-skinned guy and handed him a package and told him. "We'll be back tomorrow." as we headed for the door. Hope never uttered so much as a single word to me, and I said nothing to her. We left there headed for the Hole.

Uncle Lucky was waiting at the bar for us when we arrived. He quickly ushered us to the back room. "That's some real good dope you have there, young man. I'm tempted to buy an ounce for myself, but I know the Feds may be watching me." He chuckled as we entered the room.

He pulled out a scale and placed it on the table. I took out everything I had and placed it on the table. I pushed one of the ounces towards the scale and said, "Weigh that up and make sure it's a full ounce. I weighed it myself, so the weight is accurate."

Nitty opened the package and poured its' contents on the scale. We all smiled as we read the reading. It was exactly twenty-eight grams. Uncle Lucky suggested we try to see just how much cut the drugs could take and still be good. To my surprise Uncle Lucky pulled out a coffee grinder and plugged it in. I asked if we should be wearing masks. He laughed and answered, "Not the way I'm getting ready to show you." The statement aroused my curiosity. He was excited for the opportunity to teach me and it showed in his presentation as he proceeded with his demonstration. He placed one gram in the grinder along with four grams of lactose. "This here will tell the captain! If my man likes it with a four on it, it's a stand-up six. I can't remember the last time anything around here could stand up to anything more than a three on it."

He took out a box of Saran wrap. He cut a piece of the thin clear cellophane paper large enough to cover the cup of the grinder, which held the drugs. He carefully placed the piece of cellophane over the compartment and placed the lid into place. It became amazingly obvious to me why this would work. The cellophane was not a porous material, so it's fumes wouldn't be allowed to escape into the atmosphere. He pushed down on the top and turned on the grinder. In this capacity the grinder served as a blender.

He removed the top from the grinder but allowed the cellophane to remain in place. He pointed out the fact there was nothing foreign sticking to the paper. "This is a great sign!" he said then explained the foreign substance would have been the cut put on the drug. I was pleased to learn about the test, and the fact the cut we used was not be detectable in that way. He concluded his demonstration by insisting we allow the grinder to sit untouched for five minutes to permit its' contents to settle. After waiting for the five minutes to pass, he poured its' contents on the scale and it weighed five grams.

I pulled out my new toy and listened to their words of admiration for the piece. None of them had ever seen a silver

McDonald's spoon before. I handed the spoon to Uncle Lucky and watched as he measured out two macks. He wrapped the drugs in some aluminum foil. He went to the door and beckoned his tester to come to him. He whispered something in the tall dark-skinned youngman's ear and handed him the package he had just folded. As the guy walked away, Uncle Lucky looked over his shoulder and winked at us.

Quite a bit of time had passed before the young man eventually returned. It was obvious he was struggling to walk, and his speech was extremely slurred. He was as intoxicated as a witchdoctor and very pleased with his present state. He told Uncle Lucky it was the best he had in years! We all knew at that moment we had our work cut out for us trying to figure out just how much cut this heroin was able to stand up to.

We continued testing the drug by adding more and more lactose. We finally concluded it was able to be cut ten times and still be almost twice as strong as anything on the streets. We had stumbled across a goldmine! I had the best heroin in the city. From that point on I would be receiving a minimum return of seven dollars for every dollar I invested. Without realizing it, I had received all the necessary components to become a major distributor.

I let Uncle Lucky keep all the drugs we had put the cut on and kept the rest for myself to pass out as samples. There were a few people I wanted to get with. They were going to be amazed once they checked it out. We left Uncle Lucky in the back room and hit the streets to make some major moves.

My cousin, Fast Eddie, had a friend by the name of Tony Fontane. I had my issues with him because I didn't believe he was worthy of my cousin's unconditional loyalty. Tony was trying to establish himself as a drug dealer. My cousin was his enforcer/bodyguard. He ran a dope house on West Grand Boulevard.

Slim once robbed Tony while in the company of two of his hoes and it turned out very ugly. Tony was sitting on a loveseat. There was coffee table sitting between the love seat and a sofa. Slim sat in the middle of two of his hoes directly across the table from Tony. He had gotten angry about something Tony had said to him, so he decided to rob him. He pulled his twenty-two pistol, immediately getting the drop on Tony and ordered him not to move. There was nothing Tony could do without getting shot. He knew Slim very well, so there was no doubt in his mind about Slim shooting him without hesitation. He had a nine-millimeter pistol stuck down in the side of his pants, but it might as well had been on the other side of the moon. There was no way for him to reach it.

One of Slims' hoes was a big, beautiful, young white woman. She was sitting beside Slim smoking a cigarette. There was an ashtray on the coffee table and without thinking she rose up to dump her ashes. When she leaned forward to reach the ashtray, she blocked Slims' view for a brief second. She was actually blocking Slim's line of fire.

It was the break Tony needed. He quickly pulled his pistol and got off a shot in Slims' direction, but the slug got lodged in the woman's buttocks. Before he could get a second shot off, Slim had leaped over the wounded woman who was now lying on the table squealing in pain and landed on top of Tony.

He still had a grip on his twenty-two but was faced with the task of preventing Tony from firing the weapon his direction. He managed to get the web of his hand between his thumb and fore finger, between the cocked firing pin and the pistol's hammer. The hammer pierced his skin and prevented the weapon from firing. They both continued to fight for control of the larger caliber pistol. Slim got the barrel of the nine to point at Tony's chest and tried to get the weapon to fire but the wrong weapon fired.

Slim felt the burning of the hot bullet as it passed through his face. He knew he had to fight off the urge to collapse. The consequences of losing control of the larger caliber pistol, meant a catastrophic ending for him. They continued to struggle until eventually the nine exploded and the slug plunged into Tony's chest. He didn't lose consciousness immediately, but the wound had left him incapacitated. There was nothing he could do except watch, as Slim searched for and found his stash.

Slim made it home safely and sent one of his hoes to find me. He wanted me to treat their wounds. I have no idea why he felt I could administer medical assistance, but upon being contacted I went to him without any hesitation.

Slims' wound wasn't serious. He was hit by the smaller caliber pistol and I could see where the bullet had entered his face along his jawline. The exit wound was less than an inch beyond the entrance wound. The girl's wound, however, was much more serious. There was no exit wound and the entrance wound was bleeding profusely. I treated Slim, but I could only suggest the girl be dropped off at a nearby hospital before she bled out.

There were moments none of us was sure if Tony would survive. Fast Eddie was extremely worried about his close friend. He never left his bedside until he was certain his friend was out of danger. Tony survived and a year later he was more determined than ever to prove to everyone he was meant to thrive in the game as a drug dealer. I blamed him for getting my cousin addicted to heroin afterwards, but ultimately it was my cousin's decision. He was a grown man at the time he decided to experiment with heroin.

Tony's parents lived a few doors down the street from the bar, so I went there to see if I could get his telephone number from them. To my surprise Tony answered the door after I'd knocked. I wondered and asked him why he was there instead of his spot. He told me he Dillinger and Floyd had become partners and they were at the spot at that very moment taking care business.

That didn't add up, nor did it make any sense to me. Dillinger, and Floyd were known throughout the entire west side as stickup artist. All they did was rob and terrorize dope-houses. Dillinger was a big man. He stood about six feet three inches tall and weighed well over three hundred pounds. He was young, strong as an ox and had plenty of heart. His partner Floyd also stood about six feet three, but he had a slender body. They both had the reputation of being ladies' men.

I had never met either of them, but all that was about to change. Once Tony got a taste of the sample in his nostrils, he insisted we went to show them what I had immediately. "When we get there, let me do all the talking." he insisted. "I can get us the best deal."

The spot was an upstairs flat, and it was the first time I'd ever been inside. As we walked in the house, I saw Pig sitting in a corner gazing out of a window at the streets below. Pig was a very well-known heroin dealer. I wondered what his role was in all of this. His presence collaborated the notion that

Dillinger and Floyd were serious about the idea of getting in the heroin trade.

To my surprise they all were just as excited about meeting me as I was to meet them. They were already legends and were used to the reaction of people meeting them for the very first time. I never got used to some of the reactions people had upon meeting me for the first time. Whenever someone knew who I was prior to being introduced to me, and was extremely excited about meeting me, it always caught me unprepared. This was especially so If they were already legends or famous themselves.

They all stood up to shake my hand. Tony told them he had a new connect and passed them a mack to test. After Pig cut the mack by putting two macks of lactose on it, he snorted a small amount into each of his nostrils. That's what is known as a one on one. He then passed the colorful saucer with the drugs on it to Floyd. Floyd took a one on one also.

Dillinger asked me if it were true I would be playing basketball for Jochannan that season. "Damn!" I responded. "Yes, I am playing for Jochannan this season, but how did you find out?" I asked. "I'm an unsigned, unannounced walk-on, and I've only been to one practice." He told me he seen me leaving the recreation center where Jochannan's basketball team practices, and I was carrying my gym-bag. I thought he had heard something through the grapevine, but he had only used logical deduction to figure everything out.

Just that quickly, Floyd began feeling the true effects of the drug and found it too difficult to hold your tongue. He gave up their best bargaining position by stating, "This is some bomb ass dope. I ain't never had anything this good before. I feel dope drunk."

Pig stated, "If I hadn't put the two on it myself, I would have sworn it was some raw." Therefore, the drug had been established as a top-grade product. The only the thing left to establish was the price. "How much for an ounce?" Pig asked.

That was Tony's que. I expected him to add as much as a couple of hundreds for himself. I was only charging him one thousand five hundred dollars. Much to my astonishment and bewilderment he confidently stated, "Two thousand." I became angry because I felt he was blowing the deal, but I held my tongue.

"That's too much!" Pig protested. We might a s well stick with the people we're dealing with right now than fuck with that." No matter how much they complained about the ticket being too steep, Tony held firm to his price of two thousand dollars per ounce.

I was feeling frustrated, confused, and caught between a rock and a hard place. I was about to walk away from the deal and a potential consistent customer, all because of Tony's greed. I didn't appreciate it one bit. I began wondering what they would do to him if they knew how much he was taxing them, and Floyd rose to his feet at that very next moment. He calmly walked over to where Tony was seated. Without showing any signs of there being any ulterior motive for him to be standing near Tony, he quickly reached down and snatched the nine-millimeter pistol from the waist of his pants. He then slammed the butt of the gun down on the top of his head, all before Tony had a chance to flinch. Dillinger and Pig burst into laughter.

"That's why you'll never be nothing but a bitch!" Floyd spat in his face. It was obvious Floyd had been pushed over the edge. "If you had said one thousand six or seven hundred, we would have happily paid it." he continued.

Dillinger arose while he continued laughing. He turned towards me and said, "That's why we don't need bitch niggers in our business." He turned his attention towards Floyd and said, "Come on man, so you me and Tone can work this shit out."

We stepped into an empty bedroom for privacy. Dillinger told me, "Look man, this used to be Tony's spot but when we came up here to rob his bitch ass, we liked the set-up and realized the spot's potential." He stopped for a moment to study my face and to read my reactions, before he continued. "To make a long story short, we took it over." I burst out laughing, because I no longer liked Tony and I was sure the feeling was mutual. They both seemed to enjoy the fact I found what they had done humorous. "We also know this is your shit. Lucky has been bragging to anyone who will listen to him talk about you having the best Mexican mud he has ever come across." He paused for a moment before adding, "Give us a decent price, and we'll cut you in."

I looked from Dillinger to Floyd and back again before asking, "What ya'll know about running a spot?" Dillinger laughed and responded by telling me they knew absolutely nothing, "But that is the reason we got Pig's fat bitch ass. He's so afraid of us he'll do anything we tell him to do. We're going to let him manage the spot. We're not going to treat him bad, unless he fucks up. He'll make a lot of money and he'll be able to tell everybody he's protected by us. Everyone in this room."

I knew it was an invitation to join them. It was the highest form of flattery and I felt honored. Dillinger interrupted my thoughts when he told me, "We were going to rob every spot in the hood to eliminate the competition, but this dope is so much better than everybody's we won't have to do that. What would you charge for an ounce?"

I truly only wanted one thousand five hundred dollars for it and I told them so. "That's cheap! Especially when you take into consideration how strong it is. What percentage of the profit would make you happy?" Floyd asked. I explained how it wasn't necessary because my people make sure I'm very well compensated, but they insisted that I take at least one hundred dollars off every ounce sold and no drugs other than mine could be sold there. Dillinger, Floyd, and I became partners. When we returned to the room where we had left Tony we found him with his face still covered with blood. It was running from an open wound on the top of his head. He held a bloody towel on his head and it was obvious he was in extreme pain.

Dillinger walked over to him and kneeled, so their eyes were on the same level. He looked him directly in his eyes and said, "From now on we will take care of all the bills. If anything gets cut off without you letting us know the bill is due, by the time we're through with yo ass, you're gonna wish Slims' bullet had taken your ass out.

Floyd asked me if I could get three ounces for them that night. I knew they would want some, but I didn't expect them to want it right away. I was prepared, and I let them know I could very easily accommodate request. All I needed was the cash.

Floyd and Dillinger began pulling money from their pockets. While they were busy putting their money together, I asked for and received the telephone. I was about to sell out.

I had to call Uncle Fly and see if it were possible for us to hook up once again that night.

I recognized his voice as soon as he answered the phone and responded, "Hey Uncle Fly! I need to see you again." He was very impressed, but even more so when I informed him I wanted to buy four ounces. According to my calculations, I would be just a half of an ounce shy of having a quarter of a kilo, after Uncle Fly finished working his magic with the kibote mixture. I told him I would call him when I found a ride, but he insisted upon coming to pick me up. I told him to meet me at the Hole and ended the call. If he was walking out the door as soon as the call ended, he would arrive at the Hole in approximately twenty minutes.

"We've got it!" Floyd excitedly announced. I pulled the three ounces out I had stashed in my draws. He handed me four thousand five hundred dollars and I gave him the package. "Is it all here?" he asked. I assured him it was all there, and the one bag was different in appearance only because it was broken down into quarters. I was about to walk to the Hole, but Dillinger insisted upon giving me a ride.

Although it was a short ride, it gave me and Dillinger an opportunity to get better acquainted. We asked each other about the authenticity of the many stories we had heard about one another. Some of them were fabricated, and some of it was exaggerated. Some of them were hilarious, but most of it was quite accurate. He also warned me to prepare for growth. "You made it possible for us to start out at three ounces a day. We were buying six ounces every day and even though we couldn't put anything on it, we were still growing and making a sizeable profit. Now that we do have something we can cut, there ain't no telling how big we're gonna get. This is only the beginning. Thanks to you, we're about to get over, so we're down for you until the caskets drop baby."

I had Nitty, Red, Dillinger and Floyd on my team. With their assistance I started out making over six thousand a day. In a roundabout way, Unck had unintentionally fulfilled his promise to me. I was in the position to achieve my stated ambition of becoming the richest dopeman in the history of Newport. Uncle Fly was the connection, but it was me who was moving the product. Soon enough, everyone who needed to know me, would know me. They all will soon marvel over the overall experience of taking care of business with an ambitious young man, in control of an amazing product. It was only the beginning, but I clearly had become the newest plug.

To be continued

Printed in the United States
By Bookmasters